HUMA
Strangles Cattle V

CW00923594

The cattlemen on the r;
ghastly story of a madman, who ... ...
been roaming over the reservation, killing cattle with his
naked hands to suck their blood, and in some cases
even attacking men. No one seems to know who the
man is, nor how long he has been wandering about the
ranges. He was first seen some four or five weeks ago.
Repeated attempts have been made to capture him, but
thus far without success.

He is said to labor under the hallucination that he is a
vampire. How he manages without a weapon of any
kind to kill the cattle on which he lives is a mystery.
When found after he has left them the animals appear
to have been seized by the heads, borne to the ground
by main strength and torn to pieces by the teeth and
nails of the lunatic.

Jack Lewis, a cowboy on one of the ranches about
midway between Pierre and the Black Hills, is the hero
of the most exciting adventure with the madman yet
reported. It was nearly a fortnight ago. Lewis had been
out for several days with a party on the range and about
6 o'clock in the evening he wandered away from his
companions and dismounted for a few moments. As he
stood by his horse he was suddenly struck from behind
and hurled to the ground and nearly strangled by the
maniac. He struggled furiously, but was unable to reach
his weapon, while his assailant frothed at the mouth and
made every effort to seize the cowboy by the throat with
his teeth.

COWBOYS & MONSTERS

VAMPIRES, MUMMIES, AND WEREWOLVES OF THE WILD WEST

By John LeMay

Bicep Books
Roswell, NM

First Edition

LeMay, John.
   Cowboys and Monsters: Vampires, Mummies, and
Werewolves of the Wild West
      1. History—Pioneer Era. 2. Supernatural
      3. Folklore, Early Twentieth Century.

For my friend and fellow explorer into
the supernatural, Donna Blake Birchell

CONTENTS

INTRODUCTION   11

LIST OF
ILLUSTRATIONS

BELIEVE IN VAMPIRES.

Rhode Islanders Who Are Sure That They Do Exist.

Instances Told of Where the Living Have Been Attacked and Preyed Upon by These Representatives of an Unseen World.

A MEMBER OF THE ANTI-VAMPIRE PARTY.

INTRODUCTION

This is not a book of simple Old West ghost stories, of which there are so many that one volume couldn't possibly hold them all. As the title suggests, this is indeed a tome about tangible, supernatural monsters manifested in the flesh. Therefore, this book exists in a strange limbo somewhere between cryptozoology, the study of hidden animals, and Parapsychology, the study of the paranormal. That's because many of the beings in this book appear to be flesh and blood entities but with spiritual afflictions in many cases. While ghosts are thought to be incorporeal spirits of the dead, vampires and werewolves, by comparison, appear to be rooted in our physical plane of existence but are also aided and abetted by some malicious power from the netherworld.

Though reports of mystery animals like Bigfoot and the Chupacabra are creeping along on the road to mainstream acceptance, the same can't be said for their more antiquated brethren. Perhaps it was because they were made so popular in the works of Universal Studios and Hammer Films from the early 1930s into the 1970s and people began identifying them as fictional movie monsters instead of mythical beings possibly rooted in some grain of truth.

People in the Pioneer Period had a more steadfast belief in the supernatural than we do today. In fact, their belief was strong enough that a family in Rhode Island burned the disembodied heart and liver of their deceased daughter, who they thought was a vampire. The ashes were then given to her ill brother to drink, as it was thought this would cure him of his affliction. I am speaking, of course, of the Exeter, Rhode Island, case of 1892 involving the Brown family. None of them were vampires themselves or even plagued by one, but were being ravaged by tuberculosis and burned the aforementioned internal organs in a vain effort to ward off vampirism.[1]

Similarly, in the Southwest in the year 1878 occurred something known as the Navajo Witch Purge, where around forty people were executed under the suspicion of being skinwalkers.[2] Just think, that was forty people killed due to a very strong belief in the supernatural, similar to the Salem Witch Trials of the late 1600s.

While the stories of the Exeter Vampires and the Navajo Witch Purge did in fact occur, they

---

[1] That story didn't receive its own chapter in this book because I have plans for it elsewhere, and was also trying to adhere more so to Wild West territory best that I could.

[2] If you're reading this book, you probably already know that skinwalkers are the Native American equivalent of werewolves.

stemmed more so from a fear of the supernatural as opposed to actual, supernatural events. Mercy Brown, the suspected vampire in the Exeter case, was never seen to get up and move under her own power. Her body was simply well preserved due to the cold, and she was mistaken for a vampire. Similarly, no reports of werewolves have ever actually surfaced regarding the Navajo Witch Purge of 1878, even though skinwalker sightings are common across the Southwest today.

That said, while things like the Navajo Witch Purge are covered in this book, I did strive to find cases of actual flesh and blood fiends on the loose. Though articles on vampires and werewolves were not as common as airship tales and snaik stories,[3] I still managed to dig up quite a few, while many more tales in this book stem from oral folklore passed down from generation to generation. As usual, I'd say about half of these accounts are probably just made up. Notice I said only half, though, as evidence exists suggesting that more than a few of them might just be true.

As always, the main problems we face in examining old stories like these are that of witness credibility and yellow journalism. During the 19th Century, on slow news days, reporters might simply make up a tall tale about a crashed airship from Venus with little pink men inside or a "Hoop

---

[3] A "Snaik Story," in which snake was purposely misspelled, was one in which someone encountered some kind of giant snake or otherwise reptilian monster. Airship tales, on the other hand, were the UFO sightings of their day.

Snake" rolling its way down a hill in pursuit of a hapless victim. While those wild tales are easy to discredit, it's a bit harder when the stories are more mundane. Or when the witnesses can actually be found in the historical record as semi-reputable people. Credence is also bolstered when sightings persist over several years in the same area. Examples include the case of two separate 1895 articles detailing vampire attacks that occurred within a few months and several hundred miles of one another in the states of Iowa and Nebraska. Then there were the strange sightings of leaping phantoms that plagued the Long Island, New York, area for over fifty years off and on. Or, my favorite, how werewolf-like creatures have a strange habit of being spotted at Native American burial grounds in the Midwest for some reason.

Anyhow, whether you're a skeptic, a believer, or just someone interested in the folklore of the Old West, I hope these stories will make you consider that at least some of the time, things really do go bump in the night.

John LeMay
Roswell, New Mexico
February 2022

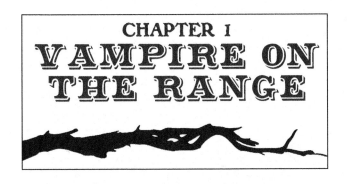

CHAPTER I
VAMPIRE ON THE RANGE

I n the spring of 1959, Universal Pictures, famous for their classic monster movies of the 1930s and 1940s, released their first Vampire Western. It was called *Curse of the Undead* and featured a typical plot where the good guys and the bad guys feud over water and land rights. However, the black-clad gunman of this film turns out to be a vampire and is defeated by a gunslinging preacher with a special crucifix bullet. Supposedly the film was a hit at the box office but considering that hardly any more cowboys vs. vampire movies followed aside from 1966's ludicrous *Billy the Kid versus Dracula*, it couldn't have been that big of a hit.

POSTER FOR *BILLY THE KID VS DRACULA.*

Oddly enough, the Old West has one literal cowboy vs. vampire tale up its sleeve, and no, it couldn't have been influenced by Bram Stoker's *Dracula.* This is because *Dracula* wasn't published until 1897, and this story appeared in newspapers in 1895. If anything, it might have been the other way around and this story could have helped inspire *Dracula* considering that Stoker was known to keep a research notebook that contained a few newspaper clippings regarding vampirism in America.

Our fantastic tale, wherein a cowboy tussles with a genuine vampire in the vicinity of the Pine Ridge territory, was published in the *Defiance Evening News* on November 12, 1895, and was still being run as late as September 24, 1896, in papers across the country. Here is the story:

HUMAN VAMPIRE
Strangles Cattle With His Naked Hands.
HIS WONDERFUL STRENGTH
Attempts to Capture Him Prove Futile.
No One Knows Who the Madman Is—
Thrilling Experience of a Dakota Cowboy.

The cattlemen on the ranges west of Pierre, S.D., tell a ghastly story of a madman, who for some time past has been roaming over the reservation, killing cattle with his naked hands to suck their blood, and in some cases even attacking men. No one seems to know who the man is, nor how long he has been wandering about the ranges. He was first seen some four or five weeks ago. Repeated attempts have been made to capture him, but thus far without success.

He is said to labor under the hallucination that he is a vampire. How he manages without a weapon of any kind to kill the cattle on which he lives is a mystery. When found after he has left them the animals appear to have been seized by the heads, borne to the ground by main strength and torn to pieces by the teeth and nails of the lunatic.

Jack Lewis, a cowboy on one of the ranches about midway between Pierre and the Black Hills, is the hero of the most exciting adventure with the madman yet reported. It was nearly a fortnight ago. Lewis had been out for several days with a party on the range and about 6 o'clock in the evening he wandered away from his companions and dismounted for a few moments. As he stood by his horse he was suddenly struck from behind and hurled to the ground and nearly strangled by the maniac. He struggled furiously, but was unable to reach his weapon, while his assailant frothed at the mouth and made every effort to seize the cowboy by the throat with his teeth.

Such wonderful strength did he display that Lewis was nearly overpowered and would doubtless have been killed had not his friends, attracted by his cries, arrived in time to rescue him. The mad man flew when he saw this re-inforcement coming, and although pursued by several men on fast horses, he contrived to elude them in the dusk and made his escape. Lewis was quite badly torn about the face and neck by the man's teeth, and received a shock from which he has not yet fully recovered.

A few researchers have called this the first Chupacabra case. As all cryptid enthusiasts know, Chupacabras do suck the blood of livestock, though they are commonly described as looking like mangy coyotes rather than vampires. That said, I did find one other case of a human vampire feeding on cattle. It was published in the *Rushford Spectator* on August 14, 1884, on page two:

> The scene of another manifestation of the superstition which ended in a tragedy was laid in Hungary. A young miller, on the eve of his marriage with a peasant girl, was suddenly seized with a mortal illness, expired, and was burned the next day. That night several cattle were killed in a mysterious manner, and the young man's betrothed dreamed that she heard him calling for help. Her story, together with the incident of the dead cattle, inflamed the minds of the villagers, already saturated with the vampire belief. They repaired in a body to the miller's grave. On opening it the supposed corpse sat up with a loud cry. The mob cried vampire, and fell upon him immediately, and beat and mangled him with stones and clubs. A Physician who examined the body shortly afterward, declared it his opinion that the young man had awakened from a trance only to be murdered by his former friends.

When I initially began researching this story, I was a bit confused by the locations in which it allegedly took place. As it was, the article came from South Dakota, but it was Nebraska that really laid claim to the story. However, Nebraska is the

---

VAMPIRE PLACE NAMES IN SOUTH DAKOTA

Unrelated to our current tale, but interesting nonetheless, are a few noteworthy vampire place names in South Dakota. Vampire Peak was named in 1915 for the many bats in the area plus the blood red streaks of sand and rock that run across the peak. Then there is also Vampire Valley, though why it was named such is unknown.

---

south-bordering state of South Dakota. Together, South Dakota and Nebraska share an area known as the Pine Ridge Territory, which extends from Northern Nebraska into Southern South Dakota.

The official Nebraska history blog wrote that the story occurred in the "northwest county of Dawes, [Nebraska] just around the Pine Ridge." Later it wrote that, "There is a report of a Jack Lewis, a cowboy working ranches around the Black Hills [South Dakota] and northern Nebraska prairie, having a personal encounter with the vampire."

The author of the article, Nebraska State Historical Society Assistant Curator Dale Bacon, passed away in 2012, so I was unable to ask him whether or not any records proving Jack Lewis's existence were ever found. Likewise, I did my best to see if I could find records of Jack Lewis in the area myself. However, that's a fairly common name, which actually makes it harder rather than easier when it comes to ascertaining the validity of a story like this. Nor did the South Dakota Historical Society Press have any knowledge of this story at all when I asked.

107—"Vampire Peak", Cedar Pass, Bad Lands Nat'l Monument, So. Dak.

108 "Vampire Valley", Cedar Pass, Bad Lands, So. Dak.

34819

VAMPIRES, MUMMIES, AND WEREWOLVES
OF THE WILD WEST

However, just as I was ready to determine that this story was one of many one-off articles with no related tales or follow-ups, I found a potentially related story. This rare tale, often missed by many paranormal enthusiasts, was unearthed by the diligent researchers of strangehistory.net. The original story was published in the *Illustrated Police News* on April 25, 1895, along with the following illustration:

A VAMPIRE.

A wealthy rancher named Converse met a horrible death at Sioux City, Woodbury co. Iowa on Wednesday. There is a maniac confined in the Sioux City Lunatic Asylum who imagines himself a vampire, and is considered excessively dangerous. A close watch was kept over him, but he managed to elude the vigilance of the guards, and escaped on Wednesday morning. Not long afterwards he met Mr.

Converse on the high road. He sprang at him in a fury, bore Converse to the ground, and literally tore him to pieces with his teeth. When Converse ceased to struggle the maniac fastened on his neck and sucked the blood from a gaping wound. He then returned to the asylum, where his shocking appearance showed the asylum officials that something dreadful had happened. Search was made, when the mangled body of the maniac's victim was discovered, mutilated almost beyond recognition.[4]

As it stands, Sioux City, Iowa, and the Pine Ridge region are roughly 350 miles apart. Could the vampire inmate of Sioux City have escaped again shortly after this article was published? And if he did, did he then flee to the Pine Ridge area where he resumed his reign of terror? The Sioux City account was published in April of 1895, and the Pine Ridge account was first published in November of 1895, giving the alleged vampire plenty of time to travel the open range.

However, that said, there's possibly a problem with the source of the Sioux City story. *The Illustrated Police News* from which it came was a tabloid as opposed to a respected news source. More than anything else, the goal of the paper was the exploitation of morbid crimes to shock readers.

---

[4] Although I was able to find this story a few different places, I would like to note that it was the user identified as "Beach Combing" who found the image from *The Illustrated Police News*.

VAMPIRES, MUMMIES, AND WEREWOLVES
OF THE WILD WEST

How much were these tales possibly embellished? Though based on real news items with lavish illustrations, it's tough to say how accurate their reports were. It was even voted the 'worst newspaper in England' by readers of the *Pall Mall Gazette*. That said, *The Illustrated Police News* is the first source of the story that we can find, but it could have appeared elsewhere first. For certain, it was afterward run in many newspapers in Australia, one of which is reprinted below.

A Human Vampire.

A WEALTHY rancher, named Converse, has met a horrible death at Sioux City, Iowa. There is a maniac confined in the Sioux City Lunatic Asylum who imagines himself a vampire, and is considered excessively dangerous. A close watch was kept over him, but he managed to elude the vigilence of his guards and escaped in the morning. Not long afterwards he met Mr. Converse on the high road. The maniac sprang at Mr. Converse in a fury, bore *him to the ground, and literally tore* him to pieces with his teeth. When Mr. Converse ceased to struggle the maniac fastened on his neck, and sucked the blood from a gaping wound. He then returned to the asylum, where his shocking appearance showed the asylum officials that something dreadful had happened. Search was made, when the mangled body of the maniac's victim was discovered mutilated almost beyond recognition.

THE LEGEND OF WALKING SAM

In trying to find other legends of the Pine Ridge area, I could find only that of "Walking Sam" which appears to be a giant, ghostly effigy of Abraham Lincoln! The seven-foot-tall phantom is a relatively recent phenomena encountered on the Pine Ridge Indian Reservation in South Dakota. The specter bears a superficial resemblance to Old Abe, and some think the name "Walking Sam" is a reference to "Uncle Sam". According to lore, Walking Sam is a spirit that fills people with so much dread and hopelessness that they commit suicide when they are alone in the woods.

As stated before, though the original source of the Iowa story is troubling, when placed in context with the better-known Nebraska tale, one has to wonder if a real vampire did ravage the ranges of the Midwest after all?

Sources:

Bacon, Dale. "Vampires of Nebraska." Nebraska State Historical Society. https://history.nebraska.gov/blog/vampires-nebraska

Beach Combing. "Iowa Vampire." Strangehistory.net. (December 28, 2017) http://www.strangehistory.net/2017/12/28/iowa-vampire/

CHAPTER 2
KING TUT'S TOMB IN THE ARKANSAS VALLEY

The idea of mummies as reanimated, bandaged corpses is mostly thanks to Universal Studios' seminal *The Mummy* (1932), in which Boris Karloff played the undead Imhotep. In real life, there are relatively few stories of mummies coming back to life from the dead. However, mummies are still indelibly linked to the supernatural, nor are they unique to Egypt and the Americas have quite a few haunted mummies of their own.

Our story begins with the mysterious civilization known as the Mound Builders. To this day, no one knows who they were, though the most popular theory says that they were giants—Abraham Lincoln even mentioned them in a speech once—while others say they were a fairly advanced race of normal human beings. Whatever they were, their culture is thought to have spanned from roughly 3500 BCE to the 16th century CE.

SPIRO MOUND PHOTOGRAPHED BY DR. ROBERT E. BELL C.1935.

These mounds extend across the Americas, but the ones we're going to discuss in this chapter are located in eastern Oklahoma. They were known collectively as the Spiro Mounds, but one in particular of special interest was alternatively known as both the Great Mortuary Mound and the Craig Mound, after one of the landowners. They stretched about 300 feet long by 100 feet wide, their highest point measuring 33 feet at the peak. It could be a coincidence, but the number 33 has a great deal of occult significance. However, considering these same mounds also aligned to the sun during the equinox much like Stonehenge, it's probably no coincidence.

SPIRO MOUND C.1935. (DR. ROBERT E. BELL)

People of the time believed that it was a burial ground for a long since vanished tribe of Native Americans. The mound was first sighted by a Choctaw named Rachel Brown, who used the nearby floodplain of the Arkansas River to grow crops. After a new barn was constructed near the mound to house mules, it didn't take long for Rachel to see that the mounds were haunted. The mules housed in the barn became so spooked and upset that they refused to work. Horses brought near the mound also became upset by something.

While spooked animals were one thing, eventually Rachel bore witness to a strange sight that would seem right at home in one of the Ghostbusters films. In 1905, Rachel was startled from her sleep by a great noise. She went to the window to peer outside and saw a great blue flame shooting from the mound. Next, she saw what she described as a tiny wagon pulled by a team of cats emerging from the fire! The cat wagons then did circles in the air around the flames.[5] Over the years, others would also claim to see the phantom wagons—but no phantom cats that I know of—which were also out of proportion, either being in miniature form or sometimes appearing gigantic.

**EXCAVATIONS AT SPIRO MOUND C.1935.
(DR. ROBERT E. BELL)**

Eventually the property came under the ownership of William Craig, who remained protective of the mounds. In 1930, Craig passed away and his heirs decided to lease the site to pot hunters. Eventually was formed the Pocola Mining Company. For two years between 1933 and 1935, the site was mined of its priceless historical artifacts,

[5] Though the culture of the Spiro Mounds was more reminiscent of Mesoamerica than ancient Egypt, I think it's worth pointing out that cats were the guardians of the Egyptian underworld.

which included carved seashells, pearls, copper breastplates and other priceless items reminiscent of Mesoamerican culture. These items were sold to museums and private collectors alike.

SPIRO MOUND C.1935. (DR. ROBERT E. BELL)

Indian Relics Unearthed In Oklahoma

Braden, Okla.—Indian relics—estimated to be from 600 to 2,000 years old and including the thigh bone of a giant brave—are being taken in large numbers from a huge burial mound 4 1-2 miles southwest of here.

The Pocola mining company, composed of six Arkansas and Oklahoma men, is in charge of excavations, begun last February.

Although it is a private enterprise, each item taken from the mound is catalogued and photographed, and careful records are being kept of the disposition of the artifacts, human bones, beads of wood and stone, pearls and large conch shells.

Situated in the middle of a field near the Arkansas river, the mound is approximately 100 feet long and 40 feet high at the peak. It is of sand, making digging comparatively easy. Excavations about 20 feet deep have been made.

Among the treasured finds is a large femur, indicating its owner must have been about nine feet tall. Bones and skeletons of other human beings are of normal size.

Charred remains, some with remnants of flesh still clinging to them, have been located, indicating the redskins of many centuries age

**EXCAVATIONS AT SPIRO MOUND C.1935.
(DR. ROBERT E. BELL)**

One day in 1935, the excavators hit a petrified mud wall 26 feet down. In *Looting Spiro Mounds*, historian David La Vere wrote, "The pick blade broke through into empty space. Immediately there was a hissing noise, as humid Oklahoma summer air rushed into the hollow chamber beyond."[6] The main chamber had an eighteen-foot ceiling, and inside they found exceptionally well-preserved mummified bodies along with other well-preserved artifacts. The bodies, still dressed in colorful garments, were of little use to the simple-minded pot hunters and were discarded.[7] Other than the mummies, the pot hunters took out every item they could get their hands on, though.

---

[6] Robert, *It Happened in Oklahoma*, Kindle Edition.
[7] Though not stated, it's possible that these mummies were giants. See the article on facing page opposite.

33

Newspapers of the time touted the discovery as "American King Tut's Tomb." The discovery of King Tut's tomb was a sensationalized event when reported in 1922 and was still fresh in the American consciousness in 1935. The story of King Tut's tomb was further immortalized when members of the expedition that uncovered it began turning up dead, pointing to the now legendary curse of King Tut's tomb.

DISCOVERY OF KING TUT'S TOMB C.1922.

And so too did a curse follow the discovery and ill-treatment of the mummies within the Great Mortuary Mound. The Pocola Mining Co. had lost several men during the excavation process, with one man being buried alive when a tunnel collapsed. While that could be chalked up to a typical mining accident, more suspicious were the deaths that occurred outside the mounds. Men were killed in car accidents and by strange illnesses, evoking shades of King Tut's Tomb. One of the lawyers representing the Pocola Mining Co. was mysteriously found dead alone in his office. The most chilling death of all was that of Reverend R.W. Wall, a local pastor who had aided Pocola Mining Co. in securing their lease. Wall was found drowned in a creek bed that had been dry for several weeks!

EXCAVATIONS AT SPIRO MOUND.
(PHIL J. NEWKUMET)

The curse apparently only extended to the careless miners of the Pocola Mining Co., though. A bit later, thanks to public outcry, the Oklahoma state legislature passed the Oklahoma Antiquities Law to protect archaeological sites and the Pocola Mining Co. got the boot. But not before dynamiting the great chamber before they left, sealing it off from a team of anthropologists from the University of Oklahoma. Humorously, they paid the curse no heed, and lead anthropologist Forrest Clements quipped, "The regular wages that come from this work—now that's something."

And indeed, no one from the anthropology department suffered the curse that we know of. Today the site is still being studied, and the ghosts seem to have been laid to rest since the days of Rachel Brown.

Sources:

Dorman, Robert. *It Happened in Oklahoma*. Globe Pequot, 2019.

CHAPTER 3
MYTH OF THE VAMPIRE TREE

According to local lore, buried in the municipal cemetery of Lafayette, Colorado, is a vampire who died in 1919. People claim that the grave is the site of much paranormal activity with spectral figures seen hanging about along with disembodied voices and strange lights. People have also claimed to have been attacked by a mysterious figure, and the only clues are a set of footprints leading back to the grave. And one of the strangest details of all: battery operated devices quickly become drained in the grave's vicinity.

And why the furor over the grave? There are two reasons. The man buried there was from Transylvania, and, also, a large tree grows from right where the man's chest would be. According to the legend, the tree grew from a stake driven through the man's heart. And why did he have a stake driven through his heart? Well, he was a vampire, of course! According to the legend, for reasons unknown, the townsfolk dug up the man's remains shortly after his burial. They saw that the man had blood near his mouth, which contained larger than normal teeth. To top it off, the man also had extremely long fingernails. And so, the townsfolk did the sensible thing and drove the aforementioned stake through his heart.

THE LAFAYETTE HEADSTONE.

Actually, two men are buried in the grave, as was sometimes the custom back then. The first man was Todor Glava, an immigrant from Austria (but born in Transylvania) who died on December 6, 1918, most likely from influenza due to the 1918 pandemic. The second man was John Trandafir, also of Transylvania, who died about a week later on the 13th. His cause of death had nothing to do with vampire lore either. (In other words, no holy water, decapitation, or stakes to the heart.) Probably also due to the 1918 pandemic, Trandafir died of pneumonia. Of the two men, it was Todor Glava who was thought to be the vampire.

LAFAYETTE, COLORADO, C.1920s.
(LAFAYETTE HISTORICAL SOCIETY)

Lafayette had been a booming mining town back in the late 1800s and early 20th Century. As such, it attracted many immigrants looking for work. When asked about the alleged vampire, Claudia Lund, curator of the Lafayette Miner's Museum, said, "Supposedly [he was] a miner that came from Transylvania. And that part of the world has always had a certain history behind it. Particularly the Dracula story and everything."[8]

As it stands, there are no stories of either Trandafir or Glava attacking the populace of

---

[8] "There's a vampire buried in Lafayette?" (KUSA, 2015)
https://www.9news.com/article/news/theres-a-vampire-buried-in-lafayette/134429175

Lafayette. The vampire legend sprang about predominantly from the tree apparently.[9] "A tree, supposedly, mysteriously grew up from the grave where his heart would have been, and people wondered if there wasn't a stake driven through his heart because they thought he was a vampire," Lund explained.[10] When blood-red roses also grew near the grave (said to be his fingernails), that was apparently all people needed to start the vampire story.

After the vampire myth was established, local children would dare each other to stand upon the grave as children do. It wasn't long after that stories started to emerge about ghosts being sighted near the grave along with strange voices being heard. One investigator, Anam Paranormal, took an EVP (electronic voice phenomena) device to record the noises near the grave and also an EMF, which detects electromagnetic fields. The results were surprising.

Anam Paranormal recorded that, "EMF ranged from zeros to maxes and never really stayed at one reading or another the whole time, so good luck getting a decent base reading for comparison. Even in the daytime, EMF went too nutty." Spookier than that, the EVP recorded a voice stating, "You want my stake?"[11]

---

[9] I would guess that the tree came first, and the legend of locals staking the dead man in his grave came after.

[10] "There's a vampire buried in Lafayette?" (KUSA, 2015)
https://www.9news.com/article/news/theres-a-vampire-buried-in-lafayette/134429175

11 https://www.anamparanormal.com/114

However, Anam Paranormal doesn't believe that the spirit residing near the grave is an actual vampire, but rather a ghost playing off the grave's reputation. An interesting theory for certain.

Sources:

Anam Paranormal. "114 - Lafeyette Cemetery - The Vampire Grave." https://www.anamparanormal.com/114

KUSA Staff. "There's a vampire buried in Lafayette?" (KUSA, 2015) https://www.9news.com/article/news/theres-a-vampire-buried-in-lafayette/134429175

PORTRAIT OF ALLEGED SKINWALKER BY
EDWARD S. CURTIS C.1904.

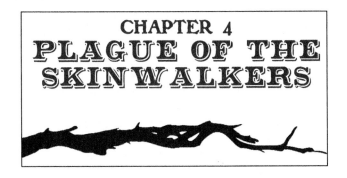

CHAPTER 4
PLAGUE OF THE SKINWALKERS

Between August of 1864 to the end of 1866 occurred the tragic "Long Walk" or "Trail of Tears." During that time, the Navajo people made an arduous trek from Arizona and Western New Mexico to the Bosque Redondo Indian Reservation in Fort Sumner, New Mexico.[12] During the course of those two years, thousands of Navajos in over fifty separate groups were forced to make the traumatic journey across the desert to Bosque Redondo. To make matters worse, they would have to share Bosque Redondo with their old enemies, the Mescalero Apache. By 1868 the endeavor was officially acknowledged as a failure, and all the Navajo were allowed to return home to

---

[12] If the place name of Fort Sumner rings a bell, that's because that's where outlaw Billy the Kid was killed in 1881.

the place they called Dinehtah, or Navajoland. But, the horrors and ramifications of the Long Walk weren't over yet, because, like many other historical events, the aftermath of the Long Walk has a hidden history veiled in the supernatural.

A U.S. CAVALRYMAN STANDS WATCH DURING THE LONG WALK.

When the Navajo returned to their homeland in 1868, they did so without adequate provisions for the journey. As such, when they settled back to what they thought would be their old lives in Dinehtah, they fell upon hard times. There was great sickness among the people and their livestock alike. Arousing suspicions, probably based upon jealousy part of the time, was the fact that some families prospered with their livestock and farms while others suffered badly. Some blamed this sickness, along with other hardships, on witchcraft. Over the next decade, the whispers of witchcraft would grow louder until they finally reached a fever pitch in the summer of 1878.

VAMPIRES, MUMMIES, AND WEREWOLVES
OF THE WILD WEST

According to the Navajo, there were four types of witchcraft that could be perpetrated, identified as witchery, sorcery, wizardry, and frenzy witchcraft. It was the middle two categories, sorcery and witchery, that made up the bulk of the allegations in the Navajo Witch Purge of 1878. Of the four categories, the middle two made up the bulk of allegations during 1878. Sorcery in the Navajo context referred to the burial of property of victims or pieces of the victims themselves, and witchery in this sense meant people being hit or injected with foreign projectiles. For instance, the bone dart is the most dreaded weapon of many Native American cultures, and it was often fired by a skinwalker.

The notorious skinwalkers are most common to the Navajo, though a few other Native American tribes have variations of them, and all could change into different animals. Or, in other words, they were Native American werewolves. Only they didn't just transform into wolves, they could also become foxes, coyotes, and other animals common to the Southwest including types of birds.

Today, "skinwalker" is a term that the layman knows the creatures by, but the Navajo themselves call them "yee naaldlooshii" or, "with it, he goes on all fours." Whereas tribal medicine men used their knowledge to heal the sick, the skinwalkers used theirs to harm and commit evil deeds. Their most powerful "medicine" was corpse powder, the dried-up, crushed bone powder of the dead. Also common were the aforementioned bone darts, fired at their victims to cause sickness.

As to how one became a skinwalker, the finer points are still shrouded in mystery for the most part, but the final phase of the initiation occurred after one had killed either a sibling or a close relative. To induce the transformation from man to beast, the skinwalker must wear the pelt of the animal they wish to transform into. Sometimes they might also wear the skull of the animal atop their heads, as it was thought this increased their power. They would pick their animal based upon the task at hand. If they wanted speed, they might choose a fleet four-footed animal like a wolf, or even a mountain lion of some sort.[13] If they wanted brute strength, they might choose a bear, for instance. For this reason, one won't see a regular Navajo wearing the pelt of a predatory animal, as the skinwalkers made it taboo.

The skinwalker's powers didn't stop at shapeshifting, they were also able to possess people. Perhaps possession isn't the right word, as it wasn't implied that their spirit entered their victim's body so much as they could gain control over a person after locking eyes with them for too long.

And how might one spot a skinwalker? Well, in human form, they are said to have animal-like eyes, while in animal form, their eyes appear more human-like and will also glow red when a bright light is shown upon them.

---

[13] *Cowboys & Saurians South of the Border* has a tale of a Skinwalker that transformed into the cryptid big cat the Onza.

ANOTHER ALLEGED SKINWALKER BY
EDWARD S. CURTIS.

Though witchcraft had always been a despised but acknowledged part of the Navajo existence, what kicked off what would later be known as the Navajo Witch Purge was the chilling discovery of a "cursed item" in the first half of 1878. Apparently, a Navajo had found the "cursed item" buried in the Arizona desert near Ganado Lake, only being a good Navajo, this person couldn't touch the cursed

item. As such, a trusted trader named Charles
Hubbell was recruited to do so. Charles was the
less well-known brother of Juan "Don" Lorenzo
Hubble, who along with his brother, was born in
San Miguel County, New Mexico. Together the
two established a franchise of trading posts across
the Southwest.

JUAN LORENZO HUBBELL.

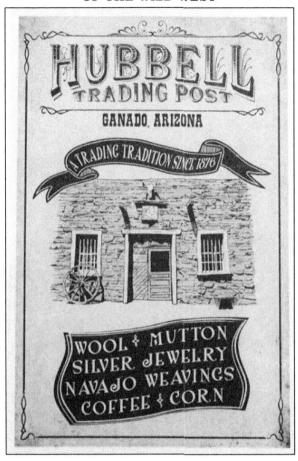

Eventually, the brothers developed quite a rapport with the Navajo and began trading with them. One of the ways in which the Hubbells benefited the Navajo (and themselves) was in helping them to determine which patterns on their blankets were the most popular among consumers so that they would know what to produce more of.

Of Hubbell, it was said that "Sentiment about him varied. Euro-Americans viewed him as the dean of Indian traders in the Southwest. Some Navajo customers said it was good to have trader Hubbell as a friend, while others said Navajos did everything around his trading ranch for low wages."[14]

---

[14] Blue, *Indian Trader: The Life and Times of J. L. Hubbell*, p.9.

As stated before, the Navajos requested that Charles Hubbell go and remove the cursed item found near Ganado Lake. Hubbell agreed and made a chilling discovery. Though accounts differ on what he found, the most interesting alleges that within a shallow grave, Hubbell found a dead body with the stomach split open. Within the stomach, he found either a curse scrawled across a random piece of paper or the actual 1868 treaty between the Navajo and the U.S. government that had released them from Bosque Grande.

A grandson of a tribal member named Hash keh yilnaya years later recollected to researcher Martha Blue that "the collection that these witches gathered was found wrapped in paper and this paper was I think the Treaty of 1868. . .buried in the belly of a dead person in a grave. . . ."[15]

The unearthing of this cursed item set about a series of events comparable to the Salem Witch Trials of the late 1600s, only much less publicized, and which resulted in an estimated 40 people being executed as skinwalkers or witches. While some of the executed persons may well have been actual skinwalkers, it is believed that plenty of others were just the victims of malicious false allegations motivated by jealousy and petty feuds.

The first skinwalker to die was executed right in front of Hubbell's Trading Post, possibly in the doorway itself. Years later, an elderly tribesman named Yazzie T'iis Yazh related the following to researcher Martha Blue:

Hastiin Jieh Kaal/Digoli was first killed in the doorway of Hubbell's first trading post near the lake after he told about his companion killing young people. After that the trading post was relocated to the present site because Navajos were afraid of the trading post where Hastiin Jieh Kaal/Digoli was slain and considered the building haunted.

---

[15] Ibid, p.9.

ALLEGED SKINWALKERS PHOTOGRAPHED
BY EDWARD S. CURTIS.

Whoever killed the skinwalker in front of Hubbell's lucrative trading post made a poor decision in location, as the Navajo belief system warns that the dead spirit of a violent killing will linger at the kill spot. As such, Hubbell moved his post to a location nearer Ganado Lake.[16] Yazh said,

....in the doorway there was blood all over, so the people living around there told [Hubbell] that he shouldn't live in a place where someone dies.[17]

---

[16] This wasn't likely due to Hubbell sharing that belief so much as he knew the Navajo held that belief and would no longer frequent his post.

[17] Blue, *Indian Trader: The Life and Times of J. L. Hubbell*, pp.8-9.

Soon after, the Navajo went after the Hastiin Jieh Kaal's companion that he had accused of killing young people. Yazh related to Blue that,

> [H]is companion was Hastiin Biwosi and was in the vicinity performing a ceremony so some Navajos went there to kill Hastiin Biwosi.[18]

According to some accounts, as many as 50 people went out in search of Biwosi. A grandson of one of the posse, Hash keh yilnaya, said that "people gathered... from Ganado, and some from Greasewood, and others from Klagetoh... they prepared themselves... armed themselves with guns, arrows, clubs... there were many people riding horses... fifty... or hundred.[19]

Where exactly the posse found Biwosi has never been specified, but find him they did in some kind of residence. They stated their business to the inhabitants of the structure, all of whom left, and the party then drug Biwosi outside. There, a respected leader of the tribe, Totsohnii Hastiin, officially pronounced Biwosi as a witch and all but one were set to kill him, that being Ganado Mucho, who cried, "[H]e's my relative... my older brother!"[20]

In some accounts, it was also stated that Mucho made the case that as dangerous as a skinwalker was in life, its ghost could be even more deadly.

---

[18] Ibid, p.9.
[19] Ibid, pp.9-10.
[20] Ibid, p.11.

However, Hash keh yilnaya argued that Biwosi had "cut off [his] chance for a good life. . ."[21] Totsohnii Hastiin then gave the go-ahead to kill Biwosi, and the group shot him and then stoned him to death.[22]

Following Biwosi's death, tensions continued to escalate throughout Dinehtah. Charles Hubbell and his employees feared that since their post had been the sight of the first killing that they may be implicated in it somehow. By late spring, Hubbell was concerned enough with the "Witch Purge" to write a letter to "W.B. Leonard, Fort Defiance, Arizona Territory, Yavapai County" on May 31, 1878. In the letter, he requested that he be sent rifles and ammunition because he was expecting a "big row" among the Navajo. Specifically, he felt that a large band of them may arrive from Canyon de Chelly, Arizona, to attack most of the Anglo settlers, and in particular, he feared for his store being destroyed.

In another letter written on the same day, Hubbell revealed he had received intel from an informant he identified only as Ganio, that certain Indians were arming themselves and had intent to harm him specifically. As such, he requested that soldiers from Fort Defiance come and protect him, his family, and their post.[23]

---

[21] Ibid.

[22] Reportedly, even Mucho participated in the killing despite his earlier protests. However, he later feared that due to his "serious transgression, the killing of a relative" that he would suffer retaliation of some sort.

[23] It is unknown if these letters was written before or after the killing of Hastiin Biwosi.

FORT WINGATE, NEW MEXICO.

Sometime later, Manuelito—another Navajo tribal leader—arrived at Fort Wingate with a letter he had written to J. L. Hubbell—stating that "the Navajos had tied up six medicine men accused of witchcraft" and that he was convinced many Navajos would start murdering each other without military intervention. As to why Manuelito himself wasn't caught up in the witch hunt, it was because his own cousin had been executed earlier that summer.

Eventually, the military intervened as requested. Ten accused witches were then brought before a military council presided over by Lieutenant D. D. Mitchell. Instead of having them executed as the Navajo would have done, he let them go and gave a stern speech condemning the wanton killing of the alleged witches. After this, the killings lessened in number, though a few still occurred in isolated areas from time to time. But, for the most part, the Navajo Witch Purge of 1878 was over.

Of course, today we brush off the 1878 witchcraft claims as pure unfounded superstition. And while most of them probably were false claims based upon petty feuds, how many more might have concerned true supernatural evil? After all, there are still many sightings of skinwalkers in Navajo country today...

Sources:

Allison, A. Lynn. "The Navajo Witch Purge Of 1878." *Arizona State University West Literary Magazine* (May 2001). www.west.asu.edu//paloverde- /Paloverde2ooi/Witch, him.

Blue, Martha. *Indian Trader: The Life and Times of J. L. Hubbell.* Kiva Publishing, Inc., 2000.

----------------------*The Witch Purge of 1878.* Navajo Community College Press, 1988.

CHAPTER 5
MINERAL POINT VAMPIRE

For most people, the tale of the Mineral Point Vampire begins on March 14, 1981. On that night, police responded to reports of a strange looking man haunting the Graceland Cemetery. According to the witness testimony of officer John Pepper, he saw what he described as "a huge person, wearing a black cape with a white painted face...... about 6' 5" and ugly." Or, in other words, Pepper encountered a classic vampire from a Hollywood horror movie from the days of Bela Lugosi and Christopher Lee. When the officer asked the vampiric-looking man what he was doing in the cemetery, the man turned and ran. Pepper was never able to catch the vampire and watched as it cleared a four-foot fence and ran into an adjacent cow pasture where Angus bulls were grazing. After the report went public, the Wisconsin town of Mineral Point went wild with rumors of a vampire. As winter turned to spring, sightings of the vampire man continued. After that flap of sightings dissipated, they resumed over twenty years later in the early 2000s with more vampire sightings.

The most terrifying sighting of all occurred along a jetty in 2008. A pair of young lovers were fishing at Ludden Lake when they heard something crawling underneath the jetty they were fishing on. When the young man aimed his flashlight at the boards beneath their feet, he spied the same pale-faced vampire man sighted back in the 1980s crawling underneath! The couple ran to their car with the caped creature in hot pursuit and they fled the area.

As an old mining settlement with Cornish roots, Mineral Point is an appropriate home for a vampire. And, as it turns out, the vampire had been lurking for much longer than initially thought, and sightings had begun back in the mid-1800s when it was known under the name of the Ridgeway Phantom. (Ridgeway is an area located between Mineral Point and Blue Mounds, by the way, so it's not far.)

Ridgeway sported a variety of paranormal activity including headless ghosts and spook lights but the most famous was always the Ridgeway Phantom. It liked to prey on lone travelers in the woodlands late at night—but then again, don't they always?

More specifically, the Ridgeway Phantom haunted what was called the old Military Road nearest the aptly named town of Pokerville in Iowa County. It haunted a 25-foot stretch of the road that spanned from Pokerville to Dodgeville, both of which were mining communities just like nearby Mineral Point.

REMAINS OF RIDGEWAY.

The area boasted no less than a dozen saloons, if not more. Ridgeway, in particular, was a wild spot with numerous fights, robberies, and murders in the area. For some reason, locals tied the origins of the Ridgeway Phantom to the murder of two teenage boys at McKillip's Saloon in 1840. The boys' names have been lost to history, but they were aged fourteen and fifteen. The younger of the two was tossed into a fireplace for reasons unknown by some evil saloon goers, while the other froze to death outside as he fled town. The boys had died by fire and ice, and somehow, someway, the Ridgeway Phantom arose from the killings and began to haunt the area soon after. Rather than looking at the different ghosts as separate entities, local lore said they were all the shapeshifting phantom. That's how the more recent Mineral Point Vampire ties in, as folks seem to think that it's the Ridgeway Phantom's modern form. And he could be if we follow the John Keel school of ultraterrestrials.

You most likely don't need a refresher on Mothman, but you're getting one anyways. As you may recall, in 1967, Point Pleasant, West Virginia, was besieged not just by the strange, winged humanoid known as Mothman, but also ghosts, UFOs, and the Men in Black all at once. Due to this, Keel began to speculate that Mothman and his kin might be a form of the older trickster myth, a being beyond our understanding that either couldn't or wouldn't communicate in a normal way. He dubbed these modern era tricksters "ultraterrestrials", the idea being that these neo-tricksters shapeshifted into a form that a witness of the era would recognize. For instance, in 19th century Ireland, ultraterrestrials might take the form of fairies, while in 20th century America they might appear as aliens and so on. So perhaps the trickster of Iowa County, Wisconsin, took on various forms over the years, starting with the spook known as the Ridgeway Phantom and eventually gave itself a makeover into something more akin to a Hollywood vampire.

And indeed, the being did have the behavior of a trickster all the way back in the mid-19th century. The website The W-Files wrote of the specter that,

> He ranged the Highway and the surrounding farmlands, playing his mischievous and harmful pranks upon travelers and inhabitants alike. He was that most exasperating of phantoms, the practical joker, and one who shamelessly exploited his obvious advantage, played according to no rules whatever, and generally turned out to be a downright nuisance.[24]

For instance, according to lore, the invisible specter joined in one of Pokerville's many poker games one night. Three miners sat playing poker, with a fourth chair left empty, and you can guess what invisible figure was really sitting in it. When one of the men won a full pot and went to grab his winnings, the cards suddenly began to shuffle themselves for the next round as though by invisible hands. Suddenly, a strange man materialized in the fourth seat, his hat pulled down partly over his face to conceal it.

The men let the stranger play with them, only odd things happened to the cards he dealt. After picking up a card, it would instantly leave the person's hand and fly around the room! Soon, a

---

[24] http://www.w-files.com/files/ghridgeway.html.

whole slew of cards was flying around the table in a circle, and the miners ran out the door.

There were several occasions where the ghost lashed people with a switch. One night two Pokerville men were carrying a plank across their shoulders down the road. A being dressed in all white suddenly leaped from the bushes, landed on the plank, and began whipping the men with a switch. They ran, and eventually the being disappeared.

In another incident, a man named John Riley was preparing to take his wagon down the old Military Road. Afraid of the ghost, he went inside to get a drink to muster his courage. When he returned, his oxen had suddenly been hitched to the rear of his wagon. In the distance, he could see what he knew to be the ghost walking away—a trickster indeed. After a while, all the area's misfortunes were blamed on the Ridgeway Phantom. These are just a few of the tales to concern the specter, which could probably fill a book of their own.

VAMPIRES, MUMMIES, AND WEREWOLVES
OF THE WILD WEST

According to at least one source, the Ridgeway Phantom was seen in flaps about forty years apart, starting in the 1840s, resuming again in the 1890s, 1930s, and 1970s. The Mineral Point Vampire seems a bit more impatient, as it popped up every ten years for a while as opposed to every forty. But what purpose do these strange ultraterrestrials serve? Do they just enjoy pranking the more primitive human race, or is there something more behind their seemingly random appearances? John Keel holds that ultraterrestrials served as omens preceding disaster. In Mothman's case, there was the Silver Bridge collapse. In South America, a glowing "terror bird" preceded a great earthquake in Peru in 1868. So far as we can tell, the Ridgeway Phantom never preceded any major catastrophes or natural disasters, but those from the Keel school of ultraterrestrials did point out that the first sighting of the Mineral Point Vampire in mid-March of 1981 preceded the assassination attempt on President Ronald Reagan later that month. Coincidence? Perhaps, but until the mystery of these spooks and so-called ultraterrestrials is solved, every bit of information serves as a potential piece of the puzzle.

Sources:

Hauck, Dennis William. *The National Directory Of Haunted Places.* Penguin Books, 2002.

ENTRANCE TO THE CAVE OF WINDS.

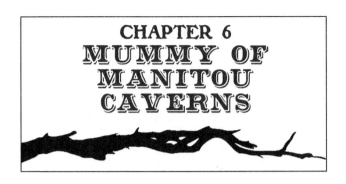

CHAPTER 6
MUMMY OF MANITOU CAVERNS

L ocated in Williams Canyon, a few miles northwest of Colorado Springs, you'll find the Cave of Winds, still one of the most popular tourist attractions in Colorado today.

According to local lore, the cave was used as a ceremonial spot for the Ute and Apache and might have served as an entrance to the underworld according to the Ute, while the Apache believed the cavern was home to a Great Spirit of the Wind. Supposedly, two schoolboys, John and George Pickett, found the entrance to the cave in 1880 and an exploration took place in June of that same year. The next year, the cave's first great promoter arrived: George Washington Snider.

GEORGE SNIDER, LEFT, ALONG WITH GEORGE AND JOHN PICKET AS ADULTS.

Snider was a stonecutter from Ohio who found and explored a different section of the cave in 1881. He labeled his new discovery Canopy Hall due to its immense size. The room was about 200 feet long and housed thousands of stalactites and stalagmites. Snider saw the possibilities of a major tourist attraction and purchased the cave land from Frank Hemenway on January 29, 1881. Unfortunately for Snider, soon after making his discovery public, hordes of people descended into the cave to strip away many of the stalactites. Eventually, Snider's investment did pay off, and not only did he operate the Cave of Winds with a partner, but also a newly discovered cave he named Manitou Grand Caverns.

Tours were conducted by lantern at the time, and on some occasions Snider even held parties in the caverns.[25] Due to the darkness of the caves, Snider took delight in finding ways to frighten his customers. Actually, this is what led to the cavern's notoriety and success. When business began to lag, Snider got the idea to place a mummy within the cavern. His brother worked at a nearby quarry which just happened to unearth three mummies, which Snider speculated were probably the bodies of Utes. Though it took days of begging, Snider finally convinced his brother to sell him one of the mummies for a grand total of $5. Snider pretended/assumed that the mummy was that of a very important Ute, and would hide it within the cave. At just the right moment, he would surprise tourists with the mummy to get a good scare out of them.

The trick worked like a charm and Snider's business was booming. After a few months, Snider was well aware that word had gotten out as to whereabouts the mummy was hidden in the cave, thus lessening the surprise. Therefore, Snider

---

[25] To light the caverns, he paid young boys five cents an hour to stand around and hold lanterns. One day, after a party was held the previous night, the mother of some missing brothers came to see Snider to tell him that her boys never came home. Snider was both disturbed and perplexed. He had keys to the entrance, and had made sure to search the cavern thoroughly before locking up. Sadly, the two boys were never found in the cave or elsewhere.

endeavored to hide the mummy in a new spot as a way of surprising a group of college athletes that had booked a tour. Remarkably, when Snider went to move the mummy, it was gone!

UNRELATED STOCK IMAGE OF THE DISCOVERY OF AN AZTEC MUMMY.

As stated before, Snider was the only one who had access to the cavern and the entrance was sealed by a locked door—a door that only Snider had the key to. Plus, he had seen the mummy the day before it vanished. As such, one has to wonder just where the mummy went? It certainly didn't get up and walk out on its own...

As stated earlier, supposedly the Ute Native American tribe considered this cavern to be an entrance into the underworld. A legend even existed that a portal would open within the cave which allowed the spirits of the dead to pass to and fro. Perhaps the mummy fell into the portal and went to the underworld where it belonged?

Whatever happened to the mummy, be it mundane or supernatural, today the caverns are haunted. Tour guides have reported seeing people within the group tours that seemed to be dressed in the styles of the 19th Century. These same "people" were not present at the beginning of the tour and disappeared by the end of it. Spook lights have also been seen within the cave. One of the ghosts is even thought to be Snider himself, along with his wife.

CAVE OF WINDS ENTRANCE C. 1950s.

Interestingly enough, on the night that Snider passed away in 1921, a severe lightning storm hit the valley. It produced a flood so intense that it caused a rockslide that sealed off the entrance to Snider's cave! The entrance remained sealed for 30 whole years. During the process of reopening and also after, the cave was plagued with bad luck—everything from odd lawsuits to freak accidents and even death. Odder yet, the cave was suddenly infested with grasshoppers and earthworms. In some cases, people disappeared into the caves never to be seen again. Due to the caves allegedly being the site of many Native American rituals, most people assume that the bad luck is attributed to that, and the mummy no doubt played a part as well.

CHAPTER 7
WEREWOLVES
OF KENTUCKY

I n the same way that Nebraska is a strange place to find a vampire, so too is Kentucky a strange place to find werewolves. That's right, werewolves plural.

We'll begin with the early 1800s era legend of Nils Wills from the Red River Gorge area. Supposedly, Wills was the first settler in that area of Kentucky and in the process befriended several Cherokee hunters. While Wills was out hunting one day, he suffered a terrible accident. Atop a high cliff, he stumbled and fell to what should have been his death. Instead, he was found in the process of dying by some of his Cherokee friends.

They brought him back to their tribe and asked the tribal elders if they could help. The elders knew of only one method, something called the "Wolf

Gift"—a strange ritual the details of which we do not know.

WEREWOLF ENGRAVING.

Wills awoke alive and well the next morning. More than that, his wounds had completely healed. But like all good fairy tales, this gift came with a terrible curse. From that day forward, Wills was essentially a Cherokee version of a skinwalker called a *Limikin*. However, unlike most Native American skinwalkers, which induce their transformation willingly, the *Limikin* changed from man into wolf involuntarily. Holding the Christian view of the evil werewolf, Wills was mortified. More than that, he was enraged. The Cherokee didn't understand—to them it was a gift—but to

Wills it was a curse. He made it his mission to kill all of the tribal elders and members who had inflicted this evil upon him. After they were dead, he even hunted down their families. Allegedly Wills killed any Native American he came into contact with until his death in 1810. Or, presumed death, I should say. To this day, when hikers go missing—or half-eaten human remains are discovered—the Wills Werewolf is still blamed.

As recently as November of 2015, something akin to the Wills Werewolf was spotted in Red River Gorge by campers. The beast was never clearly seen and the witness observed only two red eyes. The devil in the details applies to the noises the creature made, which the witness said sounded like "a large man being slaughtered combined with a wolf."[26]

Leaving the Wills Werewolf behind in Red River Gorge, we will now travel to another uniquely named location: The Land Between Lakes. The area is so named because it is located between two large lakes, those being Lake Barkley and Kentucky Lake. It has been the haunt of a seven-foot-tall werewolf known as the Beast of the Land Between Lakes for generations. There are two iterations of the legend, one European and the other Native American. The European legend goes that an immigrant family from Europe came to America in the early 1800s to settle in the land "Between the Rivers". This man supposedly carried a genetic disease that he had also passed

---

[26] http://www.kentuckybigfoot.com/counties/powell.htm

down to his children. This mysterious condition caused the family to "go mad" after nightfall. The family secluded themselves from the rest of the world and the children never went to school. Many years later, in the 1900s, their homestead was found abandoned (or, in other words, there were no dead bodies). Where they went is a mystery, but some think that collectively they are the mysterious "Beast of the Land Between Lakes".

VINTAGE LAKE KENTUCKY POSTCARD.

As for the other legend, it centers around a Chickasaw shaman who could shapeshift into a wolf. He was accused by his fellow tribesmen of using his powers for evil and cast out into the wilderness. But even that wasn't enough. Some of his tribe felt he should be killed. When not enough Chickasaw agreed to help hunt down their old shaman, the willing tribesmen uncharacteristically solicited help from drunken Anglo settlers within a nearby saloon.

The combined group went out into the wild and shot the shaman in wolf form. In his dying moments, he cursed the men and vowed to return to torment them. And, sure enough, soon after strange howls emanated from the woods, hunters mysteriously disappeared, and bison were mutilated by some hideous predator. Stranger still, livestock was occasionally discovered killed but not eaten—uncharacteristic of a predator. A few times animals were found with their legs torn from the sockets, something else a natural, known predator wouldn't have the strength to accomplish.

Eventually settlers caught a glimpse of the strange creature which resembled a wolf walking upright on two legs. Tales spread of families huddling within their cabins in fear as they listened to the creature walk across their porch. The next morning they would find deep gouges—claw marks—in the wood.

One old-timer claimed that it jumped out of one of the horse stalls in front of him one night causing him to "wet his overalls".[27] Another old-timer and his wife claimed to see it get tangled in chicken wire while trying to get into their chicken coop. Other stories are not so humorous, though. A more recent one from the 1980s claims that a murdered family was found within their camper. Well, the parents were found in their camper; the child was found half-eaten high up in a tree. Of course, if you're wondering why you didn't hear this sensational story in the news at the time, it was supposedly covered up by the local government à la *Jaws* for fear of it hurting local tourism.

However, if towns have learned anything from places like Roswell, New Mexico, or Point Pleasant, West Virginia, they should know that such stories tend to have the exact opposite effect on tourism...

Sources:

Coffey, Ron. *Kentucky Cryptids: "Monsters" of the Bluegrass State.* Fairy Ring Press, 2018.

Swancer, Brent. "The Bizarre Beast of the Land Between the Lakes." Mysterious Universe. (August 4, 2017) https://mysteriousuniverse.org/2017/08/the-bizarre-beast-of-the-land-between-the-lakes/

---

27 https://mysteriousuniverse.org/2017/08/the-bizarre-beast-of-the-land-between-the-lakes/

CHAPTER 8
A REAL INVISIBLE MAN

Stories of invisible people are rare in Fortean circles. (After all, how would you know they were there if you couldn't see them?) Furthermore, we're not talking about unseen ghosts and specters, but flesh and blood human beings that are invisible to the naked eye, just like the title character of the book made famous by H.G. Wells. So far, I have found only one notable story of such a being, which was sighted, so to speak, at 9:30 PM in New York City in the summer of 1870. Lucky for us, it predates the classic Wells story by many years.

The Providence Morning Herald reported the story of the invisible man on June 3, 1870:

A miraculous disappearance. The New York papers are exercised over the mysterious disappearance of a man, who was first noticed at about half past nine o'clock Monday evening at the corner of Twenty Seventh Street and Eighth Avenue rapidly divesting himself of his clothing. We are told that with a rapidity that seemed the work of magic, he tore off his coat, pantaloons, vest and hat and flinging these upon the sidewalk, suddenly disappeared. The street was crowded, but no one had noticed which way he went, and it really seemed as if a human being had been dissolved into nothingness, leaving nothing but his clothes to prove that he ever existed.

Even the policemen, proverbially late on all such occasions, could make nothing of the affair and after diligently searching the sewers and some excavations for buildings in the neighborhood without result contented themselves by carrying the abandoned clothes to the station house.

When I first put on my skeptic's hat to investigate this story, the first place my mind went to was the story "The Difficulty in Crossing a Field" by Ambrose Bierce. The story took place in 1854 and had a man vanish into thin air. However, though it took place in 1854, the story was published as a genuine news item for the first time in 1888. (It was later proven to be fiction, but not before inspiring several similar stories.)

FIRST EDITION OF THE INVISIBLE MAN.

The New York story listed above is different from Bierce's story, wherein the subject vanishes clothes and all into thin air. The New York story was very much like a scene from *The Invisible Man* movie of 1933 where the titular character disrobes into nothingness in the film's best remembered scene. Where then did the inspiration for this story come from?

When I looked into H.G. Wells's *The Invisible Man,* I learned that it was partly influenced by the second book of Plato's *Republic.* In that particular book, Glaucon told of the legend of the Ring of Gyges, which could make a man turn invisible. Upon doing so, the man could act with impunity and "go about among men with the powers of a god."

Was the 1870 article inspired by Plato's Republic as well, or it could it have been a genuine tale of a real invisible man?

CHAPTER 9
THE HUMAN TORCH

Pyrokinesis is the purported psychic ability of a human being to create and control fire with the mind. One of the most famous people to have this ability sprang about in the 1880s. A. William Underwood was an African American man from Paw Paw, Michigan, in his late twenties who became famous for his purported ability to start fires with his mouth. In January of 1882, a local doctor, Dr. L. C. Woodman, wrote about Underwood in the *Michigan Medical News*:

I have a singular phenomenon in the shape of a young man living here, that I have studied with much interest, and I am satisfied that his peculiar power demonstrates that electricity is the nerve force beyond dispute. His name is Wm. Underwood, aged 27 years, and his gift is that of generating fire through the medium of his breath, assisted by manipulations with his hands. He will take anybody's handkerchief, and hold it to his mouth, and rub it vigorously with his hands while breathing on it, and immediately it bursts into flames and burns until consumed.

DANIEL DUNGLAS HOME.

Though Charles Fort would later propose that Underwood had supernatural abilities, skeptics simply said that Underwood hid phosphorous in his mouth, which he spat into the handkerchief and ignited through friction. Another alleged fire-starter of the era was psychic Daniel Dunglas Home, who could also supposedly levitate. In addition to Daniel Dunglas Home and A. William Underwood, there was another lesser-known individual with similar powers. Enter Willie Brough, a twelve-year-old boy from California with a strange affliction. Unlike Underwood and Home, Brough was not able to control his abilities—and his abilities seemed much more powerful than those of the other two men. Brough's saga began in the October 8, 1886 *Fresno Republican.*

Turlock [California] comes to the front with a most peculiar mystery. It seems that a twelve-year-old boy, Willie Brough, living near Turlock, apparently sets fire to objects by his glance. On last Sunday [October 3] the phenomenon was first discovered, and the destruction of $9,000 worth of property by fire is laid to his charge—or, rather, eyes. He has recently been expelled from the Madison school near Turlock on account of his wonderful freaks. After Sunday's fire Brough's family refused to have anything to do with him, believing him to be possessed of a devil. The boy was taken in by a farmer and sent to school. On the first day there were five fires in the school—one in the center of the ceiling, one in the teacher's desk, one in the teacher's wardrobe and two on the wall. The boy discovered all, and cried from fright. The trustees met and expelled him that night. One Turlock insurance agent has given notice that he will cancel all policies on property occupied by the boy. The neighborhood of Turlock is in a furor of excitement about the mystery.

An alternate account published in *The Review and Herald* on October 26, 1886, reported that,

Willie Brough, a boy living with his parents near Turlock, California, is reported to be so charged with electricity that the snapping of his fingers causes sparks to fly. It is also stated that hay, straw, wall-paper, and other light substances burst into flame at a mere gaze from the boy, and that he had to be sent away from school owing to fires breaking out in the structure in a mysterious manner. An insurance agent will take no further risks on property in the neighborhood as long as Willie remains.

And indeed, due to the excitement, Willie and his father moved to the opposite side of the San Joaquin River to stay with relatives, as was reported in the *Electrical Review* on October 30, 1886:

Popular excitement has been so great since the story of the sinister power of Master Brough was circulated, that the father has felt impelled to move away, and has gone to reside on the other side of the San Joaquin River, taking refuge with his family in a cottage in the cotton wood timber, a long way from village or railroad. A correspondent found him there. He denied that his son had caused fires, but admitted that he had told him that when lying in bed at night he saw sparks flying about him. Willie is an extremely nervous boy, eleven years old, with a largely developed head. In a melancholy way he told the correspondent that he did not know how the mysterious fires occurred, but said he saw sparks about his own body at night. M. A. Kuhlman, who keeps a school in Mercer County, in which the alarm first began, describes how five fires broke out in one afternoon in different parts of the school-house, being caused by no visible agency. Other scholars were hastily dismissed, but Willie Brough was detained. A few minutes later he fixed his eyes on a hay shed a few yards distant and called the teacher's attention to the fact that smoke issued from the same. Very soon it was in a blaze. The teacher forbade him to come to school any more. He does not believe him guilty of arson, but is inclined to think he is a victim of supernatural agencies. On the previous Sunday eleven mysterious blazes occurred in the house of William's father. One broke out at a corner of the roof, another in some bedding in the middle of the floor and the third charred grain sacks in the barn. Willie looked at a straw stack nearby, and flames issued out of the top. The mother of the boy is prostrated with excitement and anxiety.

The saga of Willie Brough continued in the *Baltimore Underwriter* on November 5, 1886:

California's latest sensation a boy of 12 who has an eye that sets fire to every object he looks upon is a very dangerous product. It is not surprising to learn that this incendiary optic caused his occurred expulsion from a Stockton school but it is queer in this age to find rather than mischief the accepted explanation of the tricks of a bad youngster. Mysterious fires have sometimes puzzled Eastern cities but have finally been traced to a boy's hands rather than to his visional organs The poet speaks metaphorically of fire in each eye but Master Willie Brough's exploits will land him sooner in jail than in a dime museum.

Poor Willie naturally left the area and after that vanished from the newspapers. However, that was not the end of the Willie Brough saga. Lucky for us, an anthropologist and naturalist with the Sequoia Parks Conservancy, Tim Christensen, took it upon himself to collect oral histories in the area in the 1960s. One man, identified only as Roy and associated with the Masonic Lodge of Wilsonia, brought up Willie Brough to Christensen. Roy knew Brough as an adult when he worked in the Southern Sierra Nevada lumber camps. The two men became close enough that Willie admitted his secret past to Roy, notably that he had a strange uncontrollable ability to start fires.

VAMPIRES, MUMMIES, AND WEREWOLVES
OF THE WILD WEST

On a fateful day in Millwood on June 2, 1905, the black powder storage building of Camp Four of the Sanger Lumber Company exploded for seemingly no reason. However, when Willie didn't show up for work the next day, Roy knew what had happened. And indeed, Willie Brough was never seen again. Was he consumed in the fire of his own making, or did he simply skip town?

Whatever his fate, this story would appear to be true, as the odds of an old man in the 1960s making up a bizarre story based on an obscure series of newspaper articles from the 1880s doesn't seem likely.

Sources:

Swancer, Brent. "Pyrokinesis and Strange Cases of Real Life Psychic Firestarters." (April 29, 2020)
https://mysteriousuniverse.org/2020/04/pyrokinesis-and-strange-cases-of-real-life-psychic-firestarters/

"The Fire Inside Willie Brough." ESOTERX. (June 23, 2020) https://esoterx.com/2020/06/23/the-fire-inside-willie-brough/

SATAN TEMPTING BOOTH TO THE MURDER OF THE PRESIDENT.

CHAPTER 10
CURSE OF THE ASSASSIN'S MUMMY

istory tells us that on April 14, 1865, an actor named John Wilkes Booth assassinated Abraham Lincoln during a play at Ford's Theater.[28] And in that case, history would be correct. Where history becomes uncertain is upon Booth's death. According to accepted history, Booth fled on horseback towards Southern Maryland. Twelve days later, he was found within a barn on a farm in rural Northern Virginia. There he was shot through the neck and killed.

---

[28] Though General Robert E. Lee had surrendered and the Civil War was basically over, General Joseph E. Johnston was still fighting against the Union. In Booth's mind, the war wasn't over yet, and he and his other co-conspirators believed that killing Lincoln could aid the Confederacy.

FULL BODY VIEW OF THE BOOTH MUMMY.

However, much like Western outlaws Butch Cassidy, Billy the Kid, and Jesse James, there are stories that the wrong man was killed and Booth lived on. Theories abound as to why this happened, with some alleging that it was a government-endorsed conspiracy to fake Booth's death—either out of shame for not being able to apprehend him or because the government had, in fact, condoned the assassination. Whatever the case, Booth supposedly took on the alias of John St. Helen and moved to Texas, at first settling near Glen Rose before moving to Granbury, where he worked as a bartender.[29]

In 1877 in Granbury, St. Helen mistakenly believed that he was dying. On his "death bed," St. Helen confessed to a young lawyer he had worked with in the past, Finis L. Bates,[30] that he was, in fact, John Wilkes Booth. However, St. Helen pulled through and didn't die. Before fleeing Granbury, he explained to Bates that it was President Johnson himself who had authorized Lincoln's assassination. Johnson had even given Booth a special password allowing him to escape from authorities in on the plot. The man shot in the barn was just a random fugitive who was later passed off as Booth so that the real presidential assassin could slip away.

---

[29] Glen Rose and Granbury both are notable in the annals of Forteana and strange history. Glen Rose is the site of the hotly debated Paluxy River tracks where human footprints and dinosaur tracks were found imbedded in the limestone, creating quite a contradiction in the historical record. As for Granbury, it is the burial site of J. Frank Dalton, who claimed to be a surviving Jesse James! In 1976, Billy the Kid's long-missing tombstone was found in Granbury after having been stolen from Fort Sumner in 1950 shortly after a visit from Brushy Bill Roberts, a friend of Dalton's who likewise claimed to be Billy the Kid. Brushy Bill lived in Hico, Texas, not too far from Granbury. Clearly there is more to the story of Granbury being the home to presumed dead outlaws, though no one has been able to connect all the dots.

[30] Finis Bates met St. Helens when he represented him in an excise case. Bates is also famous actress Kathy Bates's grandfather.

VINTAGE POSTCARD OF GRANBURY.

Many years after his disappearance from Granbury, Booth/St. Helen resurfaced in the newspapers under the alias of David E. George. Bates just happened to read about the death of George, who committed suicide in Enid, Oklahoma, on January 13, 1903. What caught Bates's eye, naturally, was the detail that George claimed to be John Wilkes Booth!

According to the article, George had attempted suicide nine months earlier when he again thought he was dying. George confessed to the wife of a local Methodist preacher that "I am not David Elihu George. I am the one who killed the best man that ever lived. I am J. Wilkes Booth." Though the suicide attempt nine months earlier in 1902 had failed, George's second attempt did not. George had ingested a lethal amount of arsenic, which in turn also mummified his body.

DAVID E. GEORGE SHORTLY AFTER HIS
DEATH.

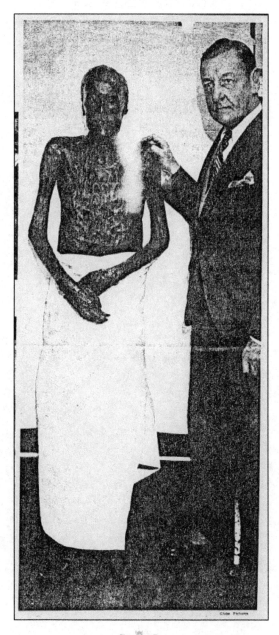

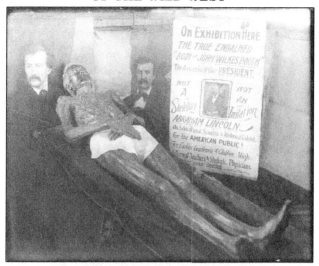

THE MUMMY ON DISPLAY.

Bates rushed to Enid upon reading the article in hopes of procuring Booth's mummified body. When he arrived, the body had further mummified thanks to the embalming fluid used by W.B. Penniman at his mortuary/furniture shop. However, Penniman himself wanted to use the unclaimed body as an attraction for his shop and refused to let Bates claim it. For several years, Booth's mummified corpse, now with glass eyes, sat upon the porch reading a newspaper. Bates found another way to exploit the wild story by writing a book, *Escape and Suicide of John Wilkes Booth: Written for the Correction of History*, in 1907. Around that same time, Bates did manage to finally procure the corpse itself. He did so with the help of an Oklahoma judge, who thought that Bates would actually bury the body since it was a former client of his. Instead, Bates rented out the notorious mummy to state fairs and carnivals. In his article on the mummy for History.com, Christopher Klein put it best when he wrote that the mummy "became a freak-show mirror image to the solemn funeral train procession taken by Lincoln's embalmed body in the weeks after the assassination."[31]

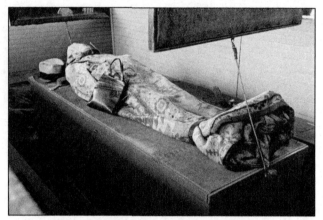

THE MUMMY UNDER WRAPS.

And like any good mummy, this one was cursed. The first inclination of the Booth Mummy's curse came when a circus train transporting the body crashed on its way to San Diego in 1920. Eight people died along with many of the so-called "freak show" animals on the train. Bates himself died not long after, and some like to claim it was due to the

---

[31] Klein, "The John Wilkes Booth Mummy That Toured America," History.com (April 17, 2015).
https://www.history.com/news/the-john-wilkes-booth-mummy-that-toured-america

ridicule he suffered from writing the book. The so-called Carnival King of the Southwest, William Evans, purchased the mummy from Bates's widow and began exhibiting it across the country as Bates had done. (Before purchasing it outright, Evans had merely been renting it from Bates.) The mummy eventually led to his financial ruin and Evans died when he was shot in a Chicago holdup in 1933.

As a *Saturday Evening Post* article published in 1938 put it, the mummy "scattered ill-luck around almost as freely as Tutankhamen is supposed to have done." The same article also stated that,

John [Wilkes Booth] has had a strange knockabout existence. He has been bought and sold, leased, held under bond, kidnapped and seized for debt; has been repeatedly chased out of town by local authorities for not having a license or for violating other ordinances; has been threatened with hanging by indignant G.A.R. veterans. Up until 1937 he has been a consistent money loser.[32]

You read that right. The Booth Mummy was at one point kidnapped and sentenced to be lynched before it was retrieved! When exactly this occurred is a bit murky. It is said it was stolen from Evans shortly after the train crash of 1920. *The Post* reported that,

---

[32] Johnston, "'JOHN WILKES BOOTH' ON TOUR,"
http://www.granburydepot.org/z/biog/BoothJohnWilkesOnTour.htm

Week after week Evans ran an advertisement in The Billboard, the Bible of the circus and carnival world, offering a reward of $1000 for information leading to the recovery of John. One day he met the alleged kidnaper on the street in San Diego. They had a knock-down-and-drag-out fight, ending in jail.[33]

There was another threat looming for the mummy. A court judge could, theoretically, insist upon the mummy's burial rather than its continued exploitation. As such, Evans really didn't want to take the kidnaper to court. Eventually, the mummy kidnapper came to Evans and told him, "I claim the reward. Pay me the $1000 and I'll return him in good condition." Incensed, but happy to have his mummy back, Evans agreed to pay $500 up front and the other $500 upon receiving the body. When he got the Booth Mummy back, he paid the kidnapper $500 via a rubber check (something akin to a hot check). So at least Evans only had to pay $500 rather than the full $1,000 for the kidnapped mummy.

The mummy received another new owner when it was purchased in 1932 for $5,000 by John Harkin. *The Post* article described Harkin as "the chief tattooed man of the Wallace-Hagenbeck circus." Having made a fortune in the circus and carnival business, Harkin invested his fortune in Chicago residential property and retired. It was likely in Chicago where he met Evans and bought

---

[33] Ibid.

the mummy off him in 1932. *The Post* reported that, "[The mummy] appealed strongly to Harkin because Harkin is a rugged individualist in his interpretation of history; he holds, for example, that Napoleon escaped after the Battle of Waterloo and that a dummy made up to resemble him was sent to St. Helena."[34]

Harkin and his wife exhibited the Booth Mummy across America in "a battered exhibition truck" which could be "converted into a small amusement palace." The Harkins apparently didn't fear the mummy, as it slept in between them on the floor of the truck (they slept in bunks on either side of it). The mummy wasn't always profitable, but it was particularly popular in Native American communities for some reason.

However, bad luck struck Harkin's real estate developments back in Chicago. It could be coincidence, of course, but most like to believe it was the mummy's curse.

Eventually, the Harkins became annexed, so to speak, by a bigger carnival operation owned by the Jay Gould Million-Dollar Show. *The Post* reported, "[Gould] is the first showman who had the genius to operate a modern American mummy successfully. After the million-dollar performance is completed, Gould steps to the loud-speaker, delivers a lecture on John, and crowds swarm to see him."[35]

---

[34] Ibid.
[35] Ibid.

Gould also remedied one of the biggest skeptical arguments against the mummy. No, not that it possibly wasn't John Wilkes Booth—that didn't seem to bother too many people—but that the mummy was real and not made of wax. *The Post* explained

Before Gould took general supervision over the attraction, its worst enemies were skeptics who would look at John and jeeringly exclaim

"Wax!" Mr. and Mrs. Harkin tremble with indignation at the mere mention of wax. Their $5000 historical and educational item has for years been up against the unfair competition of wax outlaws and heroes. Jay Gould solved this problem immediately. His first move on hitting a new town is to summon the undertakers, admit them free of charge and send them away raving. Even after decades of rough carnival and sideshow life, John is a masterpiece compared to the Pharaohs in the museums. He is as tough and leathery as a tackling dummy. One reason for this is that the Enid undertaker used arsenic in embalming the body. This is said to be the best preservative, but in recent years its use has generally been forbidden, because it may be employed to destroy the evidence in cases where murder has been perpetrated by arsenic. The fact that the suicide was by arsenic is said to have been an additional factor in preserving this mummy.[36]

The Booth Mummy continued touring the country well into the 1950s. Its history throughout the 1960s is sketchy—presumably it was mothballed for a time—and all we know is that the mummy was last seen sometime in the 1970s. Though the exact date of the last showing is never given in any sources, I did find reports that in 1977, an optometrist in Barberton, Ohio, claimed his family was in possession of the mummy. That same year,

---

[36] Ibid.

the *Sedalia Democrat* reported that the FBI was examining 18 missing pages recently found from Booth's old diary. Supposedly, these missing pages revealed much, such as that Booth claimed he was working for the secretary of war when he killed Lincoln. 1977 was a renaissance year for Booth as it even saw publication of another book detailing the theory that he survived into the 20th Century called *The Lincoln Conspiracy*. It was even made into a feature film.

Today the mummy is still missing, with reports stating that it's in the hands of a private collector somewhere. The Discovery Channel series *Mummies Unwrapped* did a segment on the missing Booth Mummy when they thought that they may have found the man who had it. The host, Ramy Romany, interviewed a man only identified as "Robert", a collector of human remains. However, to Romany's disappointment, it didn't turn out to be the Booth Mummy, but something else entirely called the "Pig-Tailed Man", which was born with a spinal deformity that gave the man a small "tail".

Much like the case of Billy the Kid and Brushy Bill Roberts, in later years there arose a cry for DNA testing on Booth's historically accepted body (i.e. not the mummy) and his brother. If the DNA matched, that would prove that Booth did indeed die back in 1865 just as the history books say. However, no DNA tests were ever conducted.

But, was the mummy really that of John Wilkes Booth? To attempt to answer that, we must return to the time when William Evans owned the mummy in the mid-to-late 1920s. At that time, Evans was approached by a Kansas City lawyer and Booth historian J.N. Wilkerson about the authenticity of the body. Wilkerson examined the mummy with Evans to look for distinctive physical traits that Booth had. For instance, Booth received a scar on his right eyebrow during a performance in *Richard III* when another actor slashed him over the right eye with the sword in the duel scene. To their shock, the mummy had the scar. Next, they sought out Booth's deformed right thumb, broken when a curtain fell on it. The mummy's right thumb was deformed. Lastly, they looked for a scar on the back of Booth's neck. It was there too.

Does this conclusively prove that the mummy and John Wilkes Booth were one and the same? Certainly not, but like his compatriots Billy the Kid and Jesse James, thanks to the mummy, the mystery of Booth's alleged in demise in 1865 still lingers to this day.

Sources:

Klein, Christopher. "The John Wilkes Booth Mummy That Toured America." History.com (April 17, 2015) https://www.history.com/news/the-john-wilkes-booth-mummy-that-toured-america

Johnston, Alva. "JOHN WILKES BOOTH' ON TOUR." *Saturday Evening Post* (February 10, 1938). http://www.granburydepot.org/z/biog/BoothJohnWilkesOnTour.htm

ILLUSTRATION FROM *HOUND OF THE BASKERVILLES* WHICH UTILIZED THE HELL HOUND LEGEND

CHAPTER II
HELL DOGS
OF EL DORADO

I n modern popular culture, relatively speaking at least, the idea of the demon dog or hellhound was probably best popularized in *The Omen* (1976). In that film, big black spectral dogs guard the antichrist in child form. Though this may have been the introduction of the hellhound for many, as you can imagine, the legend of the hellhound originated in Europe, and the most famous was that of Black Shuck.

Black Shuck made his debut during a strange thunderstorm in Suffolk on August 4, 1577. The hellish hound burst through the doors of a church,

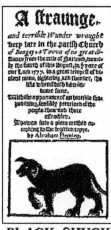

BLACK SHUCK

ran down the aisle, and killed a man and a boy. Where his paws had tread seemed to be burnt as if by fire.

The Americas have their hellhounds too. The ones most distinctive to the Old West are those said to haunt Eldorado Canyon in Nevada. The name of the canyon is ironic for a number of reasons, chief among them that it was named El Dorado canyon before gold was ever discovered there by Europeans. The Spanish named the area during their initial exploration, even though all they found there were silver veins. In the 1850s, a group of prospectors did discover gold there, and by 1858, as more people made their way up the Colorado River, the secret of the gold was out, and miners flooded the area. As such, El Dorado became one of the wildest spots of the Wild West.

In the early 1860s, a decent number of the miners comprised of Civil War deserters. Eventually, 500 men had amassed in the area to mine for gold. As usual, men killed each other either over women or gold.[37] The locale had such a lawless reputation, where killing was a daily occurrence that lawmen reportedly avoided the area and some even called it Helldorado.

---

[37] North and South tensions also resulted in some killings as well.

ELDORADO CANYON FROM THE
COLORADO RIVER, C. 1900-1925.
(UNLV SPECIAL COLLECTIONS)

Kathy Weiser said it best on Legends of America when she wrote,

Man per man and mile per mile, Eldorado Canyon has a wider range of historical events than anywhere in the Wild West. This rich history, coupled with the turbulent events taking place in Eldorado Canyon in the 19th century has led to numerous ghost stories of dead miners, Indians, and pioneers who once roamed the area.[38]

Among the most famous of Eldorado's spooks are easily the hellhounds. However, whereas most hellhounds are aligned in some way with the devil

---

[38] https://www.legendsofamerica.com/hell-dogs-of-eldorado-canyon/

and said to come from hell itself, hence the namesake, Eldorado's ghostly dogs have a unique origin all their own. Appropriately, they stem from the area's gold-boom heyday. In those days, prospectors kept vicious dogs chained up at their claim sites to protect them in the night, much like the junkyard dogs of today.

While some of these dogs may have been well-treated and cared for by their owners, according to legend, many others were not. When the miners began to leave the area in the first half of the 20th Century, many of the poor dogs were simply either shot or left staked to their chains to starve to death as they were no longer needed. The lucky ones were either taken home or released into the wild.

Today, spectral black dogs are the most commonly seen ghosts among Eldorado... supposedly. A user on the Shadowlands.net wrote of their experience in Eldorado seeing the legendary hellhounds. The author and his brother had heard of the legend and decided to explore the Eldorado region north of Hoover Dam. Their first few trips didn't yield any evidence of the dogs, spectral or otherwise. On their final visit, they found an eight-foot chain embedded into the rocks at the entrance to a mine shaft. The brothers entered the mine shaft and found the bones of a very large dog. But still, no spooks showed up. Either feeling confident that there were no ghosts, or perhaps hoping still to see one, the brothers made camp outside of the mine shaft. That night, they could hear the howls of what they assumed were coyotes when suddenly,

The atmosphere became thick and very uneasy. We now felt that we were being watched from a very close distance. What we thought was the night time breeze now sounded more like the panting or breathing of large dogs in close proximity. Then we heard the growling. Grating, low......and hatefull [sic]. The fall of paws on the desert sand now became apparent. They seemed to circle the campsite. We were surrounded.[39]

Next, the brothers' attention was drawn to a scratching noise coming from the entrance to the mine. They looked and could see the chain moving as though an invisible dog were attached to it. The chain began to tug away from the rock it was attached to while at the same time, scratch marks and blood began to appear on the rock. Finally, a hairy invisible something brushed against the author's leg. The brothers had gotten the ghostly encounter they had hoped for and promptly ran for their car. All the while, they could hear the ravenous panting and the rhythm of dogs feet pounding the dirt as they ran to the vehicle. The two men made it to their car and sped away. It was at this point that the ghostly dogs either materialized to become visible, or a live pack of dogs began following the car:

On the road heading out of the canyon we were paced for a good two or three miles at least by

---

[39] http://theshadowlands.net/ghost/ghost137.htm

what seemed to be a pack of wild strays! We made it home and I will never forget the terror of being chased by this pack of spectral hounds...NEVER![40]

While an interesting story, it is actually only one of a few as it turns out. Truthfully, not as many people claim to see these "hellhounds" of Eldorado as you might think. Or, if they do, they mostly go unreported. Apart from the account published on the Shadowlands, only one other hellhound account can be dug up that relates to Eldorado. The ever-dependable Brent Swancer of Mysterious Universe found an account on the now removed blog King Sasquatch Paranormal & Cryptozoology Blog.

The tale told of a group of friends out four-wheeling in Eldorado Canyon. One of the group saw what he took to be a coyote crouching in a "defensive stance" while his friends next to it could see no such thing (the implication being that he was seeing a ghost dog while they were not). Later that night, the shadow of a canine crept across the tent of one of the girls there, who screamed loudly at the sight of it. It is said that when she did, the animal disappeared, but the poster wasn't specific enough in their wording to clarify if he meant it ran away or faded away like a specter.

The same blog had one other account in which the witnesses were boating up the Colorado River in the vicinity of Eldorado Canyon. This account

[40] Ibid.

was a bit more interesting as it implied more of a flesh and blood cryptid rather than a ghost. The account was related by the father of one of the witnesses, who wrote,

> Around two in the morning my house phone rang off the hook with my son fanatically shouting that he had just seen a mutant dog with a piercing howl attempting to catch a duck. He forwarded the details as a four-foot mangy dog with terrifying overlapping teeth. He said the dog failed to catch ducks and ran off hungry when they shined a flashlight onto the shore.[41]

If not for its having been seen in the haunts of the hellhounds, one might well have lumped this sighting in with that of the mangy Chupacabra. Was it perhaps one of the living descendants of the prospectors' guard dogs set free into the wilds of the canyon, or did one of the spectral dogs manage to make a physical manifestation of itself?

Though sightings of these hellhounds are relatively few in number, due to their unique history, their legend has caught on quite well. They even attracted the attention of Jack Osbourne for his series *Haunted Highway* in 2102. In the episode where Jack and co. visit Eldorado Canyon, their thermal imaging cameras appeared to pick up a dog-like quadruped in the darkness, approaching one of the show's cohosts. In true *Blair Witch*

---

[41] https://mysteriousuniverse.org/2020/09/haunted-el-dorado-canyon-and-its-mysterious-hellhounds/

Project style, as the cohost runs through the desert, for a split-second, a dog-like beast is seen to jump across the screen and hit her on the shoulder and then disappear. Was it simple TV trickery or a real hellhound sighting? Considering that spooks and cryptids are loathe to show up for those actually hunting them, the former seems more likely.

Sources:

Swancer, Brent. "Haunted El Dorado Canyon and its Mysterious Hellhounds." Mysterious Universe (September 22, 2020) https://mysteriousuniverse.org/2020/09/haunted-el-dorado-canyon-and-its-mysterious-hellhounds/

Weiser, Kathy. "Hell Dogs of Eldorado Canyon." Legends of America. (updated February 2020) https://www.legendsofamerica.com/hell-dogs-of-eldorado-canyon/

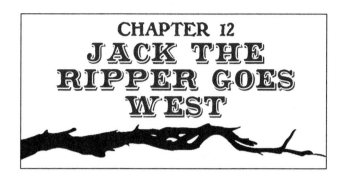

CHAPTER 12
JACK THE RIPPER GOES WEST

Arizona has some very strange ties to London, England. A good place to start is probably London Bridge, which was moved all the way from London to Lake Havasu City, Arizona. The famous London Bridge had been built in the 1830s, but over 100 years later, modern traffic was becoming too much for the structure to handle. As such, London sold the bridge to the wealthy real estate developer Robert P. McCulloch in 1968. McCulloch had the bridge dismantled and transported all the way to America for his newly created community of Lake Havasu City. Of course, McCulloch could have constructed a brand-new bridge, but he knew the famous London Bridge would help draw tourists and settlers to the area.

LONDON BRIDGE IN ARIZONA C.1972.

Today the London Bridge, successfully installed in 1971, is said to sport several ghosts recognizable to England, such as English police bobbies and so on. However, Arizona may harbor a much more famous—and monstrous—ghost in the form of none other than Jack the Ripper.[42]

RIPPER ILLUSTRATION C. OCTOBER 1888, THE ILLUSTRATED LONDON NEWS.

---

[42] Some have gone on to mistakenly tie in Jack the Ripper's ghost to the London Bridge. So far as I know, the Ripper ghost has nothing to do with the bridge and was tied into the legend for a TV movie called *Terror at London Bridge* (1985).

Jack the Ripper was infamous for terrorizing London's East End district in the year 1888. The Ripper's victims of choice were almost always prostitutes, leading some to theorize that he had a particular dislike for them. What made the killings so strange was that in at least three cases, the victims had internal organs removed. This led to speculation that the killer must have some kind of surgical knowledge. Comparable to the media frenzy that accompanied the Zodiac Killer of the late 1960s, the police were flooded by letters from people who either claimed to know the killer or were the killer. The most noteworthy of these letters, signed "From Hell", contained half of a human kidney!

Though it's uncertain that all of the killings were related, 11 murders between 1888-1891 are linked to Jack the Ripper. As the killer was never caught, no one knows what happened to him. Theories abound of course, with one of the most popular being that he succumbed to syphilis. Another account claimed that he drowned himself, and another said that he was arrested for an unrelated offense and jailed. But the most interesting theory of all claims that Jack escaped by ship to America's Wild West.

Specifically, Jack was said to settle in Benson, Arizona, a town 45 miles east-southeast of Tucson. It began life in 1880 thanks to the Southern Pacific Railroad making it a stop along their line. Primarily, Benson served as a rail junction point to ship rail freight back to the mines at Tombstone.

ANOTHER RIPPER ILLUSTRATION.

Stories of Jack the Ripper living in Benson came about in the 1930s thanks to the Federal Writer's Project (FWP). The FWP was a result of the Works Progress Administration (WPA) which gave reporters work in the form of interviewing old timers, many of which regaled reporters with tales of the Wild West. It's nearly impossible to prove some of their yarns, but if nothing else, the stories did at least come firsthand from people who lived during the time.

An unnamed man told a reporter about a stop he had in Benson the day before Thanksgiving in 1906. Due to a railroad strike, Benson was packed with "bankers, drummers, mining men, and Mexicans bound southward" as the man put it. With nothing else to do, the man frequented the saloons with his fellow stranded travelers.

In a saloon across from the railroad station was where the traveler would meet Jack the Ripper. According to him, the saloon had a roulette wheel, a big cast-iron stove, several card tables, and at the far end of the saloon was an old piano. "An immense coal-oil lamp suspended from the ceiling near the front of the room was the main source of illumination. A small oil lamp on the piano relieved the darkness of the rear," the man recollected.

The place was owned by Jesse Fisher and the principal bartender, who also acted as croupier and card dealer at times, was the man said to be Jack the Ripper. The man said that the bartender "was a character well known in southern Arizona as Jack the Ripper. His real name was unknown to most people. If you wished to attain a ripe old age, you did not ask people questions concerning their names. The etiquette of those days was very strict on this point."

On Thanksgiving morning, "Jack the Ripper ran the roulette wheel" and "the play was quite heavy" until "about one in the afternoon" when "most of the patrons left to enjoy their Thanksgiving turkey, and the games closed temporarily." Tensions began between Fisher and Jack over the measly tip the former gave to the latter. "Hell, twelve dollars is dam little for making you six hundred dollars in only a few hours—you're stingy," Jack said to Fisher.

However, Jack's temper cooled, and eventually he and Fisher left the saloon together to eat their Thanksgiving dinner. They returned at around 6 P.M., both in good spirits after having a few drinks. The bar was really booming now, with many stranded travelers there with nothing else to do. The bar was full of everyone from rowdy cowboys to saloon girls to rich Mexican landowners. Everyone seemed to be having a good time except for one man.

"The only discordant element was Jack the Ripper. Every time he passed near Fisher, he would mutter 'stingy.'" Apparently Jack was getting sore about his $12 tip again. Just as the teller of the tale was getting ready to leave, it happened:

As I started for the door I was startled by seeing Jack the Ripper produce the house gun, a big forty-five, from behind the bar. Like a chump I stopped to see what he was going to do. A few others saw him at the same time. They were more experienced. Those that could threw themselves down in front of the bar out of his sight. "Bang" went the Colt. The bullet shot out the big coal-oil lamp, causing semi-darkness. I made one grand dive for that cast-iron stove. If there had been anything larger near, I would have selected it. As fast as I was, a New York drummer was faster. He got there first and calmly tossed me back. One glance at the doorway showed me I was too late there also. It was jammed to the top. About twenty men had tried to go out at once, and they appeared piled up there like cord wood. "Bang" went the Colt again, and the chimney of the small lamp at the rear crashed. I made a second dive for the stove, but the big-nosed drummer repelled me.

Again the Colt spoke, then a man yelled and another gun joined in. It spat a fusillade, and by the sing of its slugs I knew it to be a Luger automatic, a new type of gun just appearing in Arizona at that time. Burnt powder smoke filled my nostrils. This was plainly no time to fool around without cover. Remembering my football training, I tackled low and hard and heaved the drummer into the open where he began to squeal like a stuck pig. Then I took his place behind the stove. Unless you have been in a similar situation, you will never appreciate the beauty and advantages of a big old-fashioned coal-oil burner over the little tin heater of today.

The Colt spoke again, and the Luger soon answered with a second volley. Evidently its owner had slipped in another clip. Then I noted that each "zing" of the Luger was accompanied by an ominous "zip," sounding pretty much like when you shoot into a wild bull.

By the noise from the rear I knew the door there was also jammed. There was no more shooting and the front door was soon cleared of its human dam. Not knowing exactly what might happen next and fearing the guns were simply being reloaded, I leaped outside and then stopped, standing as close to the building as I could and right beside the doorway. I correctly guessed that the near-by doorways were already filled with my late companions, who would probably welcome me much as the drummer had.

From the time the Colt was first fired, until the last Luger slug "zinged," I do not think more than twenty seconds elapsed. There must have been a full moon, for outside it was almost as light as day. There was no more shooting. Everything grew deathly quiet. I was the only person in sight on the main street. Soon a few cautious heads appeared above a stone wall across the road that separated the highway from the railroad grounds. The doorways around disgorged their occupants. Townspeople appeared and soon a great crowd collected. I turned my head before they arrived and cautiously looked inside. The interior was quite dim. The crazy little lamp on the piano was smoking badly and giving a little light, its smashed chimney strewn over the top of the piano. The moonlight helped me to see that Jack the Ripper was still at the bar, seemingly leaning over on both elbows. As I looked, he slumped over backward to the floor.

COWBOYS & MONSTERS

It happened that Harry Wheeler, then a lieutenant of the Arizona Rangers, was in town. He appeared and took charge of the proceedings. An inquest was immediately held. Then we learned that the user of the Luger automatic was Jesse Fisher. With his left hand he was holding on to the place below and behind his left hip where Jack's third shot had punctured him. It was only a flesh wound, though rather inconvenient. Jack the Ripper was dead. Fisher stated that when the Ripper shot out the lights he thought it was simply friendly fun, but when the third shot stung him where it did he felt he must stop the racket lest Jack hurt some one else. Of course all the other witnesses corroborated Fisher and he was freed on the spot. All the Luger slugs hit Jack's breast and a silver dollar would have covered the place where most of them entered. They made one big hole right through his body. Pretty good shooting in the dark!

Late the next morning I went down town—to find business going on as usual. A new bartender was on duty in Fisher's saloon. Hardly a word did I hear anywhere about the shooting of the night before. The Benson of those days had seen too many saloon killings to become excited over this little affray.

Though that is the unexaggerated tale straight from the proverbial horse's mouth, there are still some unverified elaborations. *Haunted Arizona* states an additional detail in that as Jack was dying,

Fisher finally asked him for his real name. His dying words were, "But I really am Jack the Ripper. Bury me with the knife I carry in my boot."[43]

Presumably, this treasured knife was the same one he used to commit his heinous crimes in London. Whether all this happened or not, the Ripper's ghost, knife and all, is said to haunt Benson to this day.

Sources:

Federal Writers' Project. *The WPA Guide to Arizona: The Grand Canyon State.* Trinity University Press, 2013.

Stansfield Jr., Charles. *Haunted Arizona.* Globe Pequot; Second edition (June 11, 2020)

---

[43] Stansfield, *Haunted Arizona*, p.124. [Kindle Edition]

THE ENIGMATIC COMTE ST. GERMAIN.

CHAPTER 13
SAINT GERMAIN'S IMMORTAL EXISTENCE

Of all the cities in the U.S.A., New Orleans, Louisiana, is the one most associated with vampires—and not just because Anne Rice set her novel *Interview with the Vampire* there. One of the first vampire legends to emerge there was that of the vampiric "Casket Girls", who were supposedly held captive for over three centuries in the third-floor attic of the Ursuline Convent.

The legend began in 1727 and focused on a group of girls who sailed from France to New Orleans to go under the care of the Ursuline nuns before being given away in marriage to the many new male settlers there. Because the girls traveled with curious, coffin-shaped trousseaus as luggage, they were referred to as the casket girls.

Supposedly, the girls had either knowingly or unknowingly smuggled vampires onboard the ship in their strange luggage. The vampires would sneak out at night to feed on the girls and members of the crew. Somehow, the Ursuline nuns were able to vanquish the vampires but felt too bad for the vampirized girls to kill them. And so, they locked them up in the third-story attic of the convent so that they couldn't do any harm. However, the legend is most likely just that, a legend made up long after the casket girls arrived.

NEW ORLEANS C. 1904

However, for a fact, late one night in 1903, a woman did claim to be attacked by a vampire in New Orleans. A party had just been held at the estate of wealthy socialite Jacques St. Germain at 1039 Royal Street. As several guests were leaving, a terrified woman fell from his balcony and landed nearby. The screaming woman, it was discovered, hadn't fallen by accident, she had jumped to escape the clutches of a vampire. The party-goers called for the police at once, as the girl, who it appeared might be a prostitute, continued her strange story.

She claimed that while she had been alone with Germain, he had bitten her on the neck. In between sobs, she said she only escaped because Germain had become distracted by a loud knock on the door.[44] At that point, the girl ran and jumped from the balcony, painfully breaking her legs in a few spots. When the police asked Germain about this, he passed it off on the woman being drunk. Since Germain was wealthy and respected, and the woman appeared to be a prostitute, her claims were not taken seriously. The woman was taken to a hospital, and the police asked Germain if he might come to the station the next morning to give a statement. When morning came, Germain never did. The police went to his home and found it deserted and Germain was never seen in New Orleans again.

If anyone ever fit the bill of a vampire, it was Jacques St. Germain, who had arrived in New Orleans the previous year. He was a mystery to those around him, always seen with a beautiful woman on his arm as he frequented fancy clubs and enjoyed the New Orleans nightlife. What

---

[44] An alternate version of the tale states that the girl was leaning over to gaze upon some beautiful items on Germain's mantle when he attacked her with superhuman speed and strength.

made him particularly enthralling were his stories, as Germain had apparently been everywhere. What made them odd was that Germain would speak of historical events from hundreds of years ago as though he had actually been there.

ROYAL STREET, NEW ORLEANS, AS IT WOULD HAVE APPEARED DURING ST. GERMAIN'S BRIEF REIGN OF TERROR.

What's more, Germain claimed to be the direct descendant of Comte de St. Germain, a close friend of King Louis XV who reigned from 1715 to 1774. People who compared the new St. Germain to his ancestor couldn't deny the resemblance was strong, and some even began to joke that the two were one and the same. And crazily enough, they may not have been wrong.

Once stories began to spread about Germain's uncanny resemblance to his "ancestor", his party guests began to keep a more watchful eye on him. People began to whisper about how Germain was never actually seen eating at his parties. Not only that, he didn't seem to possess any silverware of his own, as it always belonged to the catering company. The only thing that Germain partook of was drink, presumably wine, from a lavish chalice.

Odder still, the original Comte de St. Germain even claimed in his day to be hundreds of years old! And, much as the "new" St. Germain had mysteriously arrived in New Orleans, Horace Walpole, the Fourth Earl of Oxford, also noted of Comte St. Germain's mysterious nature in a letter to Horace Mann:

An odd man, who goes by the name of Comte St. Germain. He had been here these two years, and will not tell who he is, or whence, but professes that he does not go by his right name. He sings, plays on the violin wonderfully, composes, is mad, and not very sensible. He is called an Italian, a Spaniard, a Pole; a somebody that married a great fortune in Mexico, and ran away with her jewels to Constantinople, a priest, a fiddler, a vast nobleman. The Prince of Wales has had unsatiated curiosity about him, but in vain.

Supposedly, Germain refused to give his real name to anyone and only divulged it once to the King of France, Louis XV. Germain had arrived in

France in 1756 bearing gifts that he hoped could aid the French economy. Specifically, he presented the French court with vibrant dyes to use in the creation of fabrics. There, Germain blatantly claimed to have partaken in historical events that took place as far back as 500 years ago. Among his bold claims were conversations with Cleopatra and even the Queen of Sheba. Though this sounds odd for someone to reveal, back then, people were more open-minded to the supernatural.

**CAGLIOSTRO, A MYSTIC
SIMILAR TO ST. GERMAIN.**

Whether or not he ever entertained the Pharaohs, Saint Germain was friends with the likes

CAGLIOSTRO AND ST. GERMAIN

As opposed to being a vampire, some alleged instead that St. Germain had unraveled the secrets of transmutation via alchemy. This is similar to tales of the Italian mystic Cagliostro. Born Giuseppe Balsamo in 1743, the Italian occultist took on the alias of Count Allesandro Di Cagliostro. Oddly enough, this man was the inspiration behind Universal Studio's famous Mummy franchise, which began with *The Mummy* in 1932. However, that film was initially called *Cagliostro, King of the Dead.*

This is because, even though Cagliostro wasn't Egyptian, he spent several years in Egypt studying Egyptian mysticism. The enigmatic mystic claimed that he was 3,000 years old, among other things, and in 1777 he founded the Egyptian Rite of Freemasonry. By 1785, his home was ornately decorated with Egyptian symbols and his servants dressed in Egyptian robes. In 1789 he was arrested as part of the Inquisition and thrown in jail where he died... or did he? According to legend, he didn't die as no body was ever found. He simply disappeared from his cell.

Not coincidentally, it is rumored that Count Alessandro di Cagliostro met Comte de Saint-Germain. If this is true, then perhaps the two compared notes on immortality formulas? Furthermore, elite occultists have for years held that blood is the key to eternal youth, so perhaps the truth is a conflagration of both the alchemist and the vampire idea.

of Casanova, Catherine the Great, and Voltaire, who called him "a man who never dies, and who knows everything." Once, in 1760 at the home of King Louis XV's mistress, Countess von Gregory told Germain that he looked like someone she had met 50 years ago. The resemblance was so strong that she assumed Germain to be his son. Instead, Germain joked that he was over 100 years old! As they say, sometimes the best way to hide is in plain sight.

Stories alleged that Germain was part of the council of Nicaea in 325 A.D., which helped shape Christianity as we know it. More shocking still, some even claimed Germain was at the wedding at Cana where Jesus turned water into wine. Germain had many miraculous talents himself, including being ambidextrous and an esteemed linguist, alchemist, and musician. Supposedly he could precipitate diamonds from thin air and change stones into jewels. He could supposedly also manipulate metal into gold.

According to the history books, Comte St. Germain died on February 27, 1784, at the castle of Prince Charles of Hesse-Cassel. However, Germain was still sighted after his death, notably at the execution of Marie Antoinette in 1793. He was seen several times before arriving in New Orleans as well.

After the New Orleans incident, St. Germain was next sighted in Rome in 1926 by Freemason C. W. Leadbeater, who claimed that Germain told him that he currently lived in a castle in Transylvania. [45]

[45] Though no official birth records for Germain can be found, in her book *The Comte de St. Germain, the Secret of Kings*,

KEN RUSSELL'S UNMADE *DRACULA*

As some of you may know, I am also a connoisseur of lost films and unproduced screenplays. I have authored several books on the subject, one of which was *Classic Monsters Unmade*, which featured an entry on Ken Russell's un-filmed *Dracula* script from 1979. The script took a unique angle on the Count in that he is hinted to be an artist who reinvents himself once a generation. Or, in other words, around the time that he should be dead, he takes on a new alias and a new identity. I thought Russell's idea was quite novel, but now I'm not so sure that he didn't get it from the legend of St. Germain...

In his book, *The Masters and the Path,* Leadbeater claimed that Germain told him that when performing magical rituals in his castle that Germain wore "a suit of golden chain-mail which once belonged to a Roman Emperor; over it is thrown a magnificent cloak of Tyrian purple, with on its clasp a seven-pointed star in diamond and amethyst, and sometimes he wears a glorious robe of violet."

St. Germain next appeared rather appropriately on California's mystical Mount Shasta in 1930. Even in the current century in which we live, people still occasionally claim to see him.

Isabel Cooper-Oakly suggests that he was the youngest son of Prince Franz-Leopold Rakoczy of Transylvania! However, this is simply her educated speculation, not fact. In any case, it provides yet another link to the alleged vampire and Transylvania.

But was—or should we say is?—Germain really a vampire? I'll leave you with this. When the police went to his home the morning after the famous incident in New Orleans, even though they found no trace of Germain, when searching through the drawers, they found blood-stained tablecloths that appeared to have accumulated over the various parties. And as guests had always suspected, not a piece of silverware was found within the house. Lastly was found wine bottles filled with a mixture of wine and human blood...

Sources:

Crandle, Marita Woywod. *New Orleans Vampires: History and Legend.* The History Press, 2008.

Swancer, Brent. "A Real Immortal Vampire in New Orleans." Mysterious Universe (July 26, 2018). https://mysteriousuniverse.org/2018/07/a-real-immortal-vampire-in-new-orleans/

CHAPTER 14
LOBO GIRL OF DEVIL RIVER

In the Autumn of 1834, Mollie Dent mailed her parents in Georgia a rather ominous letter from Texas, where she and her husband had just moved. The short letter read:

Dear Mother,
The Devil has a river in Texas that is all his own
and it is made only for those who are grown.
Yours with love
Mollie

The rather ominous and cryptic letter referred to Devil's River, located in southwestern Texas. Mollie and her husband, John Dent, had recently moved there from Georgia, and not under the best of circumstances, either. John had been a trapper along Georgia's Chickamauga River along with a partner, Will Marlo. In 1833, John met Mollie Pertul, the daughter of some local farmers, and fell in love. Planning to marry Mollie, John needed to up his income and so quit splitting his profits with Marlo. Things escalated into a violent confrontation, and John ended up stabbing his old partner to death.

That is the reason that John and Mollie, now his wife, fled to Texas in 1834, where John began trapping beavers along the Devil's River.[46] The two lived in a brush cabin not too far away from a place now known as Carrizo Springs in the vicinity of Lake Espontosa. The area was a dangerous place, too, and a group of settlers was massacred by a tribe of Commanche, who threw the bodies of their victims into Lake Espontosa.

Eventually, John and Mollie would themselves fall victim to a massacre, but not from the Commanche... By May of 1835, Mollie learned that she was pregnant, and the couple, fearful of the nearby Commanche, decided to move to a better area known as Beaver Lake along the Devil's River.

---

[46] An alternate flourish to this story goes that Mollie Pertul was left behind by John when he went on the run, waiting for his return. Meanwhile, her parents just hoped Mollie would give up on the fugitive John and find a better suitor. Then, a year to the day that John killed his partner in April of 1834, Mollie vanished. Not only did she vanish, she had gone out to milk the cows, and in a milk pale was found the same bloodstained Bowie knife that had killed Marlo. Perhaps the bloody knife was meant to trick Mollie's parents into thinking she had been killed so they wouldn't look for her?

John built a new cabin and the family settled in. Then, on a dark and stormy night, Mollie began to go into labor. But, it was a troublesome birth, and not knowing what to do, John rode to get help from a Mexican goat ranch in Pecos Canyon. Some of the men agreed to ride back with John to his cabin, but as they mounted their horses, a lightning strike literally struck John dead.

POSTCARD OF DEVIL'S RIVER.

The Mexican farmers set out to find John's poor widow but didn't arrive until sunrise the next morning. Ominously, wolf prints surrounded the cabin. Inside, to their shock, they found Mrs. Dent dead. From the best that they could tell, she had been killed by wolves as her body bore traces of bite wounds. As for the poor baby, they could only guess that it had been devoured by the wolves. Only it wasn't.

Ten years later, at San Felipe Springs in 1845, a boy sighted a wolf pack attacking a herd of goats.

That in of itself wasn't unusual for the time. What was unusual was another form within the wolf pack that he described as "a creature, with long hair covering its features, that looked like a naked girl". Though the story was ridiculed by those that heard it, that didn't stop them from spreading it around. It was fascinating conversation, after all. A year later, a woman from San Felipe also saw the feral girl in the company of two large wolves. Together the three were feasting upon a freshly killed goat. When the woman approached, the wolves and the girl took notice and scampered away. The girl also ran on all fours for a bit before rising up on two feet like a normal human would.

With two people having seen the feral girl, area residents began to keep a sharp eye out for the Lobo Girl of Devil's River as she was beginning to be known. The Apache, too, took notice of a child's footprints and handprints mixed in with the tracks of the wolves in sandy places along the river. Mexican vaqueros (cowboys) decided to search out the poor girl, and within three days managed to sight her running with her pack along Espontosa Lake.[47] The vaqueros managed to catch the girl when they cornered her in a canyon. Having been raised by wolves her whole life, she was naturally terrified of the men and bit and clawed at them when they approached her. The men had to resort to lassoing the girl, and as they tied her up, they

---

[47] In the version of the tale published in *Straight Texas*, a folklore collection printed in 1937, it was apparently only two cowboys who cornered the girl in the canyon.

reported that she let out unearthly howls that sounded like a cross between human and animal. What was described as a "monster he-wolf" came to her rescue and attacked the men. One of the vaqueros swiftly shot it dead, and the poor lobo girl fainted.

FERAL CHILD PLAYING WITH WOLVES.

Able to examine her still form for the first time, they took note that although she was covered in unkempt hair, she was indeed human. They also took note of her well-muscled arms and legs, developed over time from running on all fours. (The men would later observe that she seemed more adept at maneuvering on all fours as opposed to on two legs like a normal human.)

The lobo girl was put on a horse and taken to a nearby ranch, where she was placed in a shack. When the men offered her a covering for her naked body, she either refused it or didn't know what it was for. The same was true of speech, for she couldn't utter words or syllables like her captors, only guttural growls. Not knowing what else to do, they left her alone.

SUNSET ROUTE, CASTLE CANYON, NEAR DEVILS RIVER, TEXAS.

That night, she howled into the darkness and her distant pack answered her. Soon the ranch was beset upon by her rescuing wolfpack, which attacked goats, cattle, and other livestock. The cowboys did their best to fend them off with guns, but in the chaos, the lobo girl tore the planks off of a boarded-up window and escaped back into the wild.

Devils River Natural Dam Resort near Del Rio, Tex.
O. F. Wyrick, Prop.

After that, no further attempts to capture the girl were made. However, the lobo girl was still sighted semi often. And it would be at this point that the sightings would take on a more fantastical, some might even say supernatural, nature. A surveying party looking for an alternate route to El Paso were riding down the Rio Grande in 1852 when they sighted the lobo woman. This time, she was suckling two wolf cubs! When she saw the men, she grabbed the cubs and sprinted into the wilderness at such a rapid gait that not even the horsemen could follow her. One version of the account, possibly from a Texas folklore collection published in 1936, stated, "In an instant she was upon her feet, a whelp under each arm, dashing into the breaks at a rate no horse could follow." Into the 1860s, sightings became infrequent, though soldiers at Camp Hudson claimed they could hear her inhuman howls in the dark of night.

Though it sounds like folklore, the saga of the lobo woman of Devil's River could be true, as tales from antiquity of orphaned children being raised by wolves are quite common. And though she was never really a werewolf, the lobo woman did eventually become a ghost.

As late as 1974, while out hunting for wild pigs (or, javalinas as they are known), a hunter named Jim Marshall and two friends sighted the lobo woman long after she should have been dead. They were camped along Devil's River and had been hunting for four days. That night, when one of the men went to gather some firewood, he returned to camp with a face as white as death. Marshall asked his friend what he had seen, and he replied that it would be better if they saw it for themselves. The two men followed their friend down a trail to the water's edge as he described the strange apparition he had seen, which looked like a young girl. Upon reaching the spot, the apparition was still there. The men later said,

The only way I can describe it is that it appeared to be a girl, a real skinny girl, with long hair and wild eyes. Even in the darkness we could see her. It was like she was in a haze, a kind of foggy mist, standing there partly bent over, digging into an ant mound. Suddenly whatever we were seeing was gone. I don't know if it vanished or just moved quickly into the brush."[48]

Supposedly, the three men returned to camp, packed up their things, and left as quick as they could.

Sources:

"Was orphan girl really raised by wolves?" Hays Free Press (February 5, 2016). https://haysfreepress.com/2016/02/05/was-orphan-girl-really-raised-by-wolves/

Humphreys, Gary. "The Wolf Girl of Devil's River." Texas Escapes (April 4, 2011). http://www.texasescapes.com/TexasFolklore/Wolf-Girl-of-Devils-River.htm

Murray, Earl. *Ghosts of the Old West.* Dorset Press, 1988.

---

[48] Murray, *Ghosts of the Old West*, p.124.

JESSE JAMES.

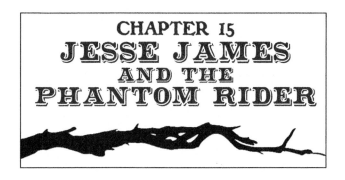

CHAPTER 15
JESSE JAMES
AND THE
PHANTOM RIDER

hough I shied away from including common ghost stories in this volume, when they involved a character like Jesse James, I thought their inclusion was warranted. Jesse James was undoubtedly one of the Wild West's best-known outlaws along with Billy the Kid, Butch Cassidy and the Sundance Kid. Some might even argue he is the Wild West's #1 outlaw.

James rode with his brother Frank, and together the two led the James–Younger Gang, which was famous for bank and train robberies across the Midwest. Over time, the James brothers were romanticized to become Robin Hood outlaws that only robbed from the rich and shared some with the poor, though today this is mostly just thought to be a myth. The gang had a decade-long heyday lasting from 1866 to 1876 which ended after a disastrous robbery attempt in Northfield, Minnesota when several gang members were either captured or killed. Though James would continue to operate up until his death in 1882, his exploits weren't quite as legendary as those committed during his glory days of the 1870s.

ALLEGED PHOTO OF THE JAMES GANG.

Something rarely reported on in terms of Jesse James lore is that of the Phantom Horseman, which James spotted at least twice during his lifetime. Some even speculated that the ghostly figure was a premonition warning of his death. According to an article on the Phantom, the story was told by Frank James shortly after his own surrender in October of 1882. The account was first published six years after the demise of Jesse and the incarceration of Frank in 1888. I'm not sure how widespread the story was, but this version was retrieved from the Wisconsin *Wood County Reporter* on October 11, 1888:

FOLLOWED BY A PHANTOM.

The Guardian Spirit of the Jesse James Family. Signaling Danger by an Appearance on a White Horse in the Moonlight - Shooting at a Ghost - Death and Danger Ever in His Track - A Strange Story.

It may not be generally known that the James family has a banshee. Yet such is the fact, and the phantom horseman that frequently appeared to Jesse James is as much a part of the traditions of that bold night rider as many of the more current incidents in his wild career.

The story of the phantom horseman was first related by Frank James to Orth H. Stein, when the two were prisoners and for a time cell-mates in the jail at Independence. It was just after the surrender of Frank James, when he was awaiting trial for the Blue Cut and Winston train robberies in this county. Stein was awaiting the outcome of a motion for a new trial after a jury had found him guilty of killing George Fredericks in this city and assessed his punishment at twenty-five years in the penitentiary. Through the intricacies of law and the uncertainties of juries, both were afterwards released. During their long and tedious confinement, however, they were wont to while away the hours with stories of their respective careers.

It was due to one of these recitals that the writer learned that the James family, and particularly Jesse, had a peculiar banshee in the shape of a white horse and phantom horseman, who appeared to warn them of danger. Although reluctant to taciturnity to speak of any matters connected with his earlier life, Frank James has since admitted that Jesse possessed the firmest faith in the omens brought by the visits of this phantom.

The story of the phantom horse which guided Jesse on his way warned him of impending danger, and finally foretold of his death, is also believed in by Mrs. Jesse James and Jesse James, Jr., the son of the deceased outlaw, who have more than once heard him speak of the visitations of this strange phantom. The last time the dead outlaw saw this phantom was just before his death, and it appeared in such a horrible shape and with such evident warning in its mein, that even the nerves of this grim outlaw were shaken, and he was weighed down at once with a sense of his impending doom.

Frank James' simple description of the appearance of the phantom horseman is as follows.

"One night we were riding along a lonely road in Tennessee. It doesn't matter just when it was or where. Jesse and I were riding along ahead, a little in advance of the rest of the party. There were five or six in the party. Suddenly we came to a broad open space where two roads met and branched off in three different directions. We emerged from under a heavy cloud of overtopping foliage into a broad flood of moonlight. It had been very dark in the woods under the heavy trees, and the bright moonlight lying thick and golden on the broad, dusty, new roads, fairly dazzled us for a moment. There, standing directly in front of us, as if to dispute our passage, clearly defined in the bright moonlight, was the figure of a horseman on a white horse. We drew rein and stood for a moment stock still. The figure in the road did not move. The moonlight shone directly on his dark coat, with bright, shiny buttons of some kind - brass or pearl - and glimmered on the silver trappings on the horse's bridle. Jesse was the first to recover himself, and, with lightning-like rapidity, he drew his gun with an oath.

"'What do you want there?' he said.

"The figure did not move or speak.

"'My God, don't shoot,' cried one of our party. 'It's a ghost.'

"Jesse's revolver went off at the same moment.

"The figure raised one of its hands, pointing the index finger at Jesse, while at the same time the horse turned and horse and rider galloped off up the road.

"'I have seen him before,' muttered Jesse, as he turned his horse in the other direction."

It is said that one of these men who was a witness of this strange encounter - the man who cried "don't shoot" - was Bill Ryan. Ryan is now doing time in the Missouri Penitentiary. Frank James who was probably less superstitious than Jesse or most of the other companions of the James boys, never took as much stock in Jesse's ghost, as the boys called it, as the great head of the outlaws and his rough-riders did. He admits, however, that Jesse was haunted by a phantom horseman, or fancied he was, until the day of his death. Jesse was always furious if anyone questioned the authenticity of his ghost.

Frank was once asked: "Do you think that was a ghost you saw that night or a man Jesse shot at and missed, or failed to kill?"

"I don't know," was the reply. "Jesse seldom missed at less than ten yards distance. Anyway, that was the first time I saw the phantom horseman."

Mrs. Jesse James, who lives on Prospect avenue, in this city, is a ladylike looking woman, who still seems to mourn for her husband. On being questioned, she had heard Jesse speak of a phantom horse which followed him about, forewarning him of danger. The appearance of the phantom foreboded evil, but Jesse generally managed to avoid evil by taking the warning in time.

Jesse James, Jr., only heir of the great land pirate, was more communicative. Jesse, Jr., is fifteen years of age, and - strange irony of fate - works for T.T. Crittenden and his sons, for that very Governor of Missouri who hounded his father to death and deceived his uncle Frank after the surrender of the latter. The story of the boy's engagement to work in Crittenden's real estate office is worth a short diversion. The boy, it appears, answered an advertisement for an office boy. Half a dozen eager applicants were there before him. Crittenden asked him what he could do.

"I'll fight, run a foot race or write a letter with any of these kids for the job," answered the brigand's son.

"Write a letter," said Crittenden.

Jesse compiled, and proved to write with a better hand than any other applicant.

"What is your name?" asked the ex-Governor kindly.

"Jesse James, Jr.," answered the boy.

Doubtless ex-Governor Crittenden was surprised to find that he was about to hire the son of the notorious Jesse, whom he had hired the assassins to kill, as the boy and his mother were to learn that the former's employer's was the ex-Governor.

But to return, as the novelist says. The boy was disposed to be quite communicative in regard to the phantom horseman.

"Dad first saw that horse in Kentucky," said the boy. "Twan't in Tennessee at all. I've heard my mother tell about it, and I've heard dad tell about it. One night the man on the phantom horse jumped up behind dad. The ghost left his horse and jumped up on dad's. Dad was with another man riding along in Kentucky. Dad rode as hard as he could and fired his pistol behind him, but he couldn't shake the ghost off until he had gone one half a mile. The thing then dropped off.

"Another time when we was all over at Kearney," continued the lad, "dad saw the ghost come in the yard on horseback and shot at it seven or eight times, but could not hit it."

This is the story of the phantom horseman as told by the family and companions of Jesse James. Did this dim shadow follow the striken brothers along the harrowing road from Northfield, Minn., taunting them with a pseudo prospect of deliverance? Was it with them in their shadowy night rides about Kansas City, when more than once they appeared and disappeared as mysterious as the phantom horseman himself?

No one can tell, for on such subjects the lips of the survivors are sealed.

- St. Louis Globe Democrat.

Despite this article's allusion to the ghost being some kind of guardian figure or omen to the family, it seemed to me to just be a ghost that popped up at random. For instance, in the story about the gang encountering the ghost at a crossroads, it might make a difference if the ghost altered their route, but if it did, no mention is made of it. Nor is their mention of Jesse seeing the ghost directly before his death. So, while Jesse may indeed have had a reoccurring phantom, how it somehow predicted his end is unclear.

Only slightly more illuminating is this shorter article, published before the other in the *Butler*

Weekly Times on August 29, 1888. It alluded to
the ghost being someone that Jesse had known
when they were still living and featured a slightly
different version of the crossroads encounter:

Jesse James and the Phantom Horseman

The story of the phantom horseman was always
firmly believed by the companions of Frank and
Jesse James. Frank was always the least
superstitious of the men who rode with the
celebrated raiders. Jesse, however, had a strong
vein of superstition in his composition and firmly
believed that the phantom horseman was his own
peculiar banshee. He frequently asserted that the
appearance of the apparition was intended as a
warning or foreboded evil. The first time Frank
James saw the apparition was one night when he,
Jesse, and several other members of the outlawed
nightriders were riding.... As they emerged from
the heavy shadows of the trees, where the two roads
met, they came upon an open space where the
moon shone brightly on the converging cross
roads. There, distinctly outlined in the bright
moonlight, sat a man on a coal black horse. The
moon shone brightly on the polished trappings of
the steed. Horse and rider remained motionless as
if silently challenging the right of the party to the
way. Jesse drew his revolver to fire, but was stopped
by the exclamation of one of the party, who
exclaimed: "My God, it is a ghost!" The figure
remained motionless and seemed to gradually fade
away before their eyes as Jesse turned his horse and

took the other road. "I've seen him before, " said Jesse, but refused to offer any further explanation. It is said that several other members of the so-called James gang have seen the phantom, among them Bill Ryan and Dick Little, and can vouch for the authenticity of this account. The phantom was generally alluded to as "Jesse's ghost, " and is said to have appeared to him shortly before his death. Jesse seemed to recognize the phantom as the ghost of somebody he had known in life, but was strangely silent on the question and never vouchsafed any explanation.

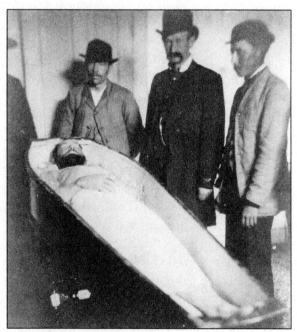

JESSE JAMES POSTMORTEM.

Whether the phantom was some kind of omen or not, Jesse James was shot dead by "the coward" Robert Ford, a new member of his gang, on April 3, 1882. James was straightening a picture on the wall of his home when Ford shot him dead through the back of the head.[49]

WOODCUT OF THE JAMES ASSASSINATION.

Naturally, in later years, it was determined the old James house was haunted. Some claimed to simply hear the sounds of phantom hooves pounding the ground while others heard gunshots accompanied by cries of death. Others observed spook lights within the home, though to my knowledge, the

---

[49] It would be remiss not to mention that, like Billy the Kid, several men popped up claiming to be a still-living Jesse James long after his death, the most notorious of which was J. Frank Dalton. Oddly enough, Dalton is buried in the same Texas town, Granbury, where a surviving John Wilkes Booth allegedly tended bar! (See Chapter 10)

man himself, Jesse James, has never been seen there. Instead, Jesse seems to be at work doing his part to promote tourism at several local inns and taverns. Today, Jesse's ghost is said to haunt the Old Talbott Tavern in Bardstown, Kentucky. Selma's St. James Hotel in Alabama likewise claims to play host to Jesse's ghost. Actually, it's not just Jesse, but even one of his old girlfriends and his trusty black dog that haunts the hotel. Whether he haunts said locations or not, one has to wonder if he also goes for a ride with the old Phantom Horseman in the ghostly netherworld every now and again.

FRANK JAMES GIVING TOURS AT THE JAMES FAMILY FARM.

CHAPTER 16
BEFORE THE BEAST OF BRAY ROAD

Thanks to the Beast of Bray Road, Wisconsin is probably the place in the U.S. today most associated with werewolves. Though it has been sighted for generations, the Wisconsin werewolf didn't become popular until the late 1980s when it was encountered along Bray Road in Walworth County. The sightings were then made famous by Linda Godfrey's reporting and her ensuing 2003 book *The Beast of Bray Road*. About 80 miles northwest of Bray Road took place the lesser-known account of the "Werewolf of Springfield Corners" in the mid-19th Century. The tale concerned an itinerant German dance instructor named Herr Gross.

VINTAGE WEREWOLF ENGRAVING.

VAMPIRES, MUMMIES, AND WEREWOLVES
OF THE WILD WEST

When strange deaths began plaguing the area of Springfield Corners, located at a crossroads northwest of Madison, locals turned a suspicious eye to Gross, who had come to the area sometime before the year 1848. Among the mysterious happenings was a housewife who saw a wolf-like monster outside. The shock made the woman fall and twist her ankle, and she claimed that the wolf laughed at her. Following this were the deaths of children, which, though due to an illness, were still blamed on witchcraft by a werewolf! A bit later, a farmer was killed on the way to Madison to buy a new horse. Though he was likely just killed by a robber to steal his gold coins, the death was still blamed on the werewolf. However, this story doesn't end with Gross being taken away and burned at the stake, as the days of the old Spanish Inquisition were long gone. Instead, locals simply whispered and spread rumors about Gross, who most likely was not a werewolf. As to the beast seen by the housewife, it would seem to be unrelated to the other incidents that plagued the area.

The next possible recorded werewolf sighting in Wisconsin occurred in 1867 in the vicinity of Oak Creek. I say possible werewolf sighting because some think this may have been a sasquatch or basic "wild man" as they were known in those days. I, however, take note of how the man-beast ran on all fours, and being in Wisconsin, one has to wonder if it was a werewolf. The story was published in the *Portsmouth Journal of Literature and Politics* on August 31, 1867:

The Milwaukee Sentinel tells a strange story about a man-beast, lately discovered in the vicinity of Oak Creek, Wisconsin. For some months the farmers in that neighborhood had been annoyed by the disappearance of their fowls. Doors were

opened and roosts were robbed in the most summary and mysterious manner; and sometimes even lambs disappeared.

That these were not stolen by human hands was thought to be evident from the marks around of the fowls being eaten on the spot. One farmer determined to solve the mystery; and so, rifle in hand, he watched his premises.

At about 11 o'clock he discovered an animal of some kind approaching his hen house with stealthy step, sometimes going on all fours, and sometimes erect. He fired, and a piercing shriek, like that of a human being, showed that the creature had been hit. It nevertheless made off to the woods, where it was seen the subsequent day, having the face and hands of a human being and the hairy body of a beast. But though wounded it made its escape, and though subsequently seen again, had not been captured at last accounts.

About fifty miles to the north of Bray Road, in the vicinity of Deerfield, Wisconsin, a werewolf sighting occurred one afternoon in December of 1896.

It came courtesy of the December 20, 1896 *Milwaukee Sentinel* and was labeled as "A Ghost Story Told by Widow Olson". I found it in Jerome Clark's *Hidden Realms, Lost Civilizations, and Beings from Other Worlds,* partially reprinted on page 204.

The story goes that the widow Olson and her 14-year-old son were living along the shores of Stump Lake when they heard a knocking on their door one day. They opened it to find a mysterious boy asking for directions to the house of a farmer who lived across the lake. As the walk to the residence was about three miles, Mrs. Olson told her son to ferry the boy across the lake to save time.

VAMPIRES, MUMMIES, AND WEREWOLVES
OF THE WILD WEST

Out on the waters of the lake is when things got weird. According to the article, the passenger sat at the stern of the boat facing away from young Olson, who tried to engage the boy in conversation to no avail, as the strange boy sat in silence. Clark reprinted the following portion of the article, and I shall do the same:

His strange behavior made Olson observe him more closely and the more closely and the more he looked at him, the more did he appear unlike a human. His attention was first attracted by the stranger's ears, which were abnormally large, reaching almost to the top of his head, where they came to nearly a point or sharp angle and were covered with a fine downy hair. His head was small and angular, something like that of a dog and covered with short, black curly hair that hugged the skin tightly. The hands were small, shriveled and covered with hair similar to that on his ears. Young Olson was now becoming almost frightened out of his wits at being alone in the boat with such an unearthly looking being and rowed with all his might. On arriving at the opposite landing he got out of the boat hastily to let out his uncongenial passenger. The stranger arose to leave the boat, but instead of facing about to walk out, he backed and carefully kept his face from view.

The rattled young Olson rowed back home as fast as his arm and oar would take him. The moment he was inside the house, he began to tell his mother about his bizarre adventure. She looked over to him to see if he was serious, and as she did so, her glance fell over into his shoulder and out the window behind him. There, running up a hill close to the house, was the strange boy last seen on the other side of the lake, though he could not possibly have made the return trip anywhere nearly that quickly. The stranger was chasing the Olson's sheep.

Mother and son both made after him, but on arriving at the crest of the hill nobody was to be seen, while the sheep stood down the slope a little way huddled together as if recently chased by a wolf or dog. There was nothing within eighty rods that the stranger could have hid behind. Why they did not notice his strange appearance before starting in the boat, how he got back so quickly and where he disappeared to, was more than the frightened widow and son could have been able to account for and they firmly believe there are still a few left of the old time elf family.

Though Mrs. Olson seemed to think of the strange boy as an elf or fairy-type being, I look at this story through the lens of lycanthropy considering that he returned to chase the family's sheep. After all, what would an elf be doing chasing sheep? And, with the many werewolf tales tracked down by Linda S. Godfrey over in the years in Wisconsin, perhaps this one should be added to the list.

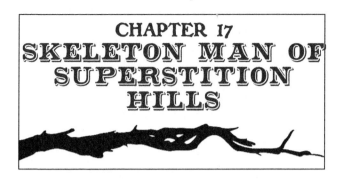

CHAPTER 17
SKELETON MAN OF SUPERSTITION HILLS

In Mesoamerica and the Hispanic Southwest is celebrated a unique holiday called the Day of the Dead. According to folklore, on the first of November (yes, the day after Halloween) the dead return to the world of the living for a visit. As such, people will set up shrines in memory of their loved ones and many more will dress up as skeletons.

A real-life skeleton-man supposedly walks the aptly named Superstition Hills of California. Located in Southern California in the Colorado Desert, this area is not to be confused with the better-known Superstition Mountains of Arizona. At an unspecified point in the past, an old prospector by the name of Charley Arizona was making camp one night about four miles southeast of Borrego. In the night, he was awoken by strange noises. Getting up to investigate, he spied a glowing object, which he at first took to be a torch or lantern. The prospector simply assumed someone was lost in the desert and was making their way towards his camp. But as the figure got closer, Charley saw that it was no living being, it was one of the undead.

SUPERSTITION HILLS, CALIFORNIA.

What he saw was essentially an eight-foot-tall skeleton man, with a light emanating from its ribcage. Lucky for Charley, the being simply walked past him and disappeared into the night. The sighting could be passed off as a one-off ghost tale if not for the fact that others in the Superstitions also saw this being. This time, two prospectors caught sight of the phantom. Their story was the same as Charley Arizona's, as they saw a light in the distance. When it came near enough, the men could make out the form of a skeletal being. A year later, another man saw the creature and told all about it at Vallecito Station. From here, legends of the Borrego Phantom, as it came to be known, would spread. Parties of spook hunters and thrill-seekers began camping in the area in hopes of spotting the phantom, and supposedly a few did. One man shot at the ghostly figure as it stumbled across the desert, and another party took to trailing it one night but lost it in a valley.

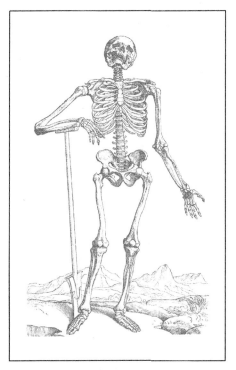

Today, many believe the phantom is simply the ghost of a prospector, but others think the creature is no ghost, but a living being of some kind. In his book *The Inhumanoids*, author Barton M. Nunnelly dubs such entities as Skeletoids, and many of them have been sighted since antiquity to the modern era. Be it a tangible being made of pure bone or a spectral phantom, always beware of the Superstition Hills of California near Borrego either way...

CHAPTER 18
WATROUS WEREWOLF

In Northern New Mexico is a small community called Watrous. In the time before Anglo-settlement, the Watrous area was a crossroads, or junction, where many different Native American tribes met to trade, including the Comanche, Kiowa, Apache, Ute, and the Puebloans. What eventually came to be known as Watrous sprang from the Santa Fe Trail in the mid-1800s. Initially, it was called La Junta. Upon the arrival of Mora County farmer and trader Samuel B. Watrous, the area began to grow due to him building a large trading post. As you can guess, eventually La Junta came to be known as Watrous. Today the area is sparsely populated with a population of only 135, though it does have the distinction of being a National Historic Landmark District.[50]

WATROUS, NEW MEXICO.

According to Jack Kutz's landmark book, *Mysteries and Miracles of New Mexico,* Watrous was once the home of several skinwalkers. Unfortunately, Kutz doesn't say when these stories took place, but since both seem to be Spanish folktales, one might presume it was the early 1800s.[51] The first story goes that one night, past midnight, a young man "whose name no one remembers now" was riding his horse down a

---

[50] The settlement began its steady decline upon a 1910 fire that nearly burned down the entire town. The Great Depression of the 1930s sounded Watrous's true death knell and by 1950 the population had dwindled to around 250 people.

[51] Kutz included the story in his chapter entitled "Open Doors to the Spirit World". Our only indication is that the story took place pre-1885, as the story followed an entry on a murder from 1885 which Kutz implies this story pre-dates.

The death of Samuel B. Watrous, though not related to the werewolf of this chapter, is interesting nonetheless as an aside. To this day Watrous's death remains unsolved. He was found near his home with two gunshot wounds to the head, which newspapers oddly supposed were self-inflicted. (How could one shoot one's self in the head twice?) Watrous's own son had committed suicide before that, and Watrous was naturally despondent over the fact and so the papers said he committed suicide himself with the very same gun. However, others think that not only was the elder Watrous murdered, but so was his son.

lonely road. The man had been visiting his cousin on a farm outside of town, and the two had stayed up late talking until they lost track of time, hence his late-night journey.

The lonely road was flanked on either side with plowed fields. His ride was uneventful until he came to a grove of cottonwood trees. Somewhere in the grove, he could hear a baby crying.[52] He dismounted his horse and looked around the area until he found a baby mysteriously hidden among the weeds. The man came to the abandoned baby's rescue, intending to take it back into town with him. When he approached his horse with the infant, the animal became upset. The man eventually calmed

---

[52] The baby crying warrants a relative aside in the lore of the skinwalker, as it is said that skinwalkers will imitate the sound of a baby crying to lure well-meaning people out to help what they assume is an abandoned infant. However, this story goes so far as to have the wicked being assume the form of a baby, which is a new one as far as I can tell.

his horse and climbed atop it with the baby in one arm.

As the horse trotted back to town, suddenly the baby spoke in the voice of a man. It told the rider that it didn't like riding this way and asked to be placed behind the man on the saddle. Terrified and not knowing what else to do, the young man moved the baby behind him onto the saddle. It clutched his waist with its tiny hands, which then supernaturally began to grow larger. At the same time the horse became panicked, and the rider did everything he could to bring it back under control. The rider was so distracted that he could hardly notice the hands getting bigger and the weight of his saddle growing heavier. As he felt the presence behind him growing larger, he heard something that sounded like the panting of an animal. He could even smell its noxious breath. At that point, he finally looked down at his waist. The tiny baby's hands had been replaced with hairy claws.

With dread, he turned his head to look behind him and saw a humanoid beast that he described as half-human and half-panther. When it shrieked, tellers of the tale embellished that the young man could hear "the screams of all the tormented souls in hell." [53]

The horse reared up in terror and succeeded in knocking off his master, but not the beast which was causing it so much panic. The young man watched from the ground in horror as the monster clung to his horse's back. Now he was able to get a

---

[53] Kutz, *Mysteries and Miracles of New Mexico*, p.86.

better look at it. Like a panther, it also had a tail which he described as "whip-like" and also "long tangled hair." (Was he referring to the hair of its head or the whole body? Kutz doesn't specify.)

The young man watched helplessly as the horse and the monster ran off into the night. The man ran in the opposite direction, back to his cousin's home, where he told his terrifying tale. According to the legend, the cousin wouldn't have believed him if not for the man's badly torn jacket. The horse was never found and the monster disappeared forever.

Though this is clearly just a folktale, the Watrous area apparently had a penchant for supernatural animal stories. This one, too, comes courtesy of Kutz, who again doesn't specify the year. He only says that it was another tale to come from Watrous. Unlike the panther monster earlier, this one is more in line with typical werewolves and skinwalkers.

For a few nights once per month, the denizens of Watrous were terrorized by a black dog. It would slink into town on dark, moonless nights. There it would target and kill dogs belonging to locals. After a few nights of terror, it would disappear and not resurface until the following month. Eventually the townspeople set out to capture the sinister animal. The next time that the moon entered its darker cycle, the townsfolk hid in the shadows to wait for the dog.

Just as they hoped, it sauntered back into town. They sprang on it and beat it with ax handles and chunks of firewood.[54] (The fact that no one tried to shoot it seems to suggest this was the earlier village of La Junta rather than the town of Watrous.) The dog wasn't killed and ran off into the wild.

The next morning, it was business as usual in the town except for one thing: an old woman that lived on the edge of town had yet to be seen. Concerned for their elderly neighbor, several people went to check on her. Inside her home, they found her bruised and beaten nearly beyond recognition.

This folktale was likely an offshoot of one from the Sonora region of Mexico, where an elderly witch turned into a mountain lion every night to terrorize local children.[55] The witch/mountain lion folktale likely made its way up north via the Hispanic settlers of the region, which was probably also true of the other folktale. The only question I have is why did Watrous of all places have several folktales that seemed inspired by the skinwalker legend?

Sources:

Kutz, Jack. *Mysteries and Miracles of New Mexico.* Rhombus Books, 1988.

---

[54] That they beat the dog with an ax handle as opposed to the sharpened tip of the ax itself was rather telling. After all, if they had chopped it up with an ax and killed it, the story would lack the exciting ending of the old woman who was apparently unbeknownst to them a witch.

[55] You might be shocked to know that the usually reliable J. Frank Dobie infamously passed the Sonora skinwalker story off as real in one of his articles.

CHAPTER 19
VICTORIAN ERA ANDROID

Believe it or not, the idea of automatons, or self-possessed intelligent machines, was not an invention of 20th Century science fiction. It was first dreamed up in Greek mythology (think Talos in *Jason and the Argonauts*). Alexandria in ancient Egypt took it a step further and began attempting to build such machines. Chinese chronicles even tell of emperors being fooled by realistic-looking robots posing as humans. "Spirit Moving Machines" was the name given to automatons in Hindu mythology, and some were said to guard the ashes of Buddha. Believe it or not, even the more learned men of the Victorian era believed in the possibility of creating a Spirit Moving Machine. Or, for lack of a better word—and in the interest of an exploitive title—an Old West era robot monster!

Enter John Murray Spears, born in Boston in 1804 and pictured to the left. Spears was many things including a spiritualist and also an abolitionist. He was part of something called the Universalist Church of America, which more or less believed that either no one was going to hell forever, or that if they did, it would only be for a limited time. This strange church begat Spears' interest in spiritualism outside of what was the norm at the time.

In 1852, Spears broke away from the Universalist Church of America for something even more radical. Spears began communicating with the dead, and not just any dead, but Benjamin Franklin, Thomas Jefferson, Emanuel Swedenborg, and John Quincy Adams among others. He called this group the "Association of Electrizers" and believed that they were guiding him to create a new, divine technology to benefit mankind.[56] And by divine, they meant divine as in a machine that would be the Second Coming!

In 1853, Spears had more or less established his own cult of followers. In a simple wooden shed atop High Rock Hill in Lynn, Massachusetts,

---

[56] The group also gave Spears visions of airships, computers, and self-sustaining cities.

Spears and his people began to create the "New Motive Power" which would hopefully usher in Utopia for mankind. Over the course of nine months, and at a cost of $2,000, they constructed the contraption.[57] The basis, or foundation, of this mystical machine was a simple dining room table atop of which sat a strange apparatus made of copper, zinc, and magnets.

OLD POSTCARD FEATURING HIGH ROCK TOWER.

In a book published at the time, *The Educator*, Spear's co-author A.E. Newton gave a firsthand account of the machine:

Upon the centre of an ordinary circular wood table, some three feet in diameter, were erected two metallic uprights, six or eight inches apart; between these, and reaching from the one to the

---

[57] About $50,000 in today's money.

other, near their tops, was suspended on pivots a small steel shaft, which was crossed at its centre by another shaft, about six inches in length, on the extremities of which were suspended two steel balls enclosing magnets. The first-named shaft was nicely fitted with sockets at its extremities, so that the balls could revolve with little friction. Beneath these suspended balls, between the uprights, and in the centre of the table, was ... a sort of oval platform, formed of a peculiar combination of magnets and metals. Directly above this were suspended a number of zinc and copper plates, alternately arranged, and said to correspond with the brain as an electric reservoir. These were supplied with lofty metallic conductors, or attractors, reaching upward ... In combination with these principal parts were adjusted various metallic bars, plates, wires, magnets, insulating substances, peculiar chemical compounds, etc., ... At certain points around the circumference of the structure, and connected with the centre, small steel balls enclosing magnets were suspended. A metallic connection with the earth, both positive and negative, corresponding with the two lower limbs, right and left, of the body, was also provided.

Spears believed that when it was complete, it would be able to move under its own power due to being imbued with a divine spirit. Around this time, one of Spears' followers, known to history only as

Mrs. Mettler,[58] claimed that she had visions foretelling that she would be "the Mary of a New Dispensation."[59] Not only that, the woman claimed she was experiencing the symptoms of pregnancy even though she wasn't pregnant. Spears sent for the woman, who came and sat with the machine for two hours, during which time she claimed to experience labor pains.

On June 29, 1854, the *New Era* published details of the strange birth:

> It was announced to Mrs. M., by spiritual intelligence, several months since, that she would become a mother in some new sense; that she would be 'the Mary of a new dispensation.' The announcement was given under circumstances the most impressive, and in connection with a most beautiful and instructive vision, in which was strikingly elucidated a most important spiritual lesson, namely, the true significance of the cross, as an emblem of spiritual advancement. All who were present on the occasion were deeply impressed with the superior capacities and exalted moral attainments of the intelligences communicating, as evidenced by the profound and comprehensive character of their teachings.

---

[58] Others say she was Sarah Newton—the wife of one of Spear's followers.

[59] Stories of secret societies influenced by demonic spirits, sometimes posing as beings of light, to create a body for the Anti-Christ to inhabit aren't all that uncommon and this is simply one of the odder examples.

Nevertheless, the prophecy or announcement spoken of, though declared with marked emphasis, and directed to be put on record, was not believed to have any peculiar meaning. It was thought to refer possibly to the maternal feeling which she had felt toward individuals, who had, through her instrumentality, been instructed in the truths of the new philosophy. Least of all was there the slightest hint that it had any relation whatever to the mechanism then constructing at High Rock. No one connected with that enterprise was present, and nothing was known of this declaration by them until it was recalled by the events which subsequently transpired. Previously to this, Mrs. M. had for some time experienced certain sensations and agonies similar to those attendant upon gestation. Subsequently these indications gradually increased, until they at length became very marked and inexplicable, and presented some very singular characteristics. They were supposed, however, to be at least partially indicative of disease; but were not imagined to have the remotest connection with either the mechanism at High Rock, or with the prophecy which has been alluded to. As the crisis approached, a variety of singular events, from apparently independent causes (which cannot be narrated here), seemed to point to some unusual result, though all failed to give any person cognizant of them the slightest apprehension of the nature of that result.

VAMPIRES, MUMMIES, AND WEREWOLVES
OF THE WILD WEST

At length a request came, through the instrumentality of J.M. Spear, that on a certain day she would visit the tower at High Rock. No one in the flesh — herself least of all — had any conception of the object of this visit. When there, however (suitable preparations having been carefully made by superior direction, though their purpose was incomprehensible), she began to experience the peculiar and agonizing sensations of parturition, differing somewhat from the ordinary experience, inasmuch as the throes were internal, and of the spirit rather than of the physical nature, but nevertheless quite as uncontrollable, and not less severe than those pertaining to the latter. This extraordinary physical phenomenon continued for about the space of two hours. Its purpose and results were wholly incomprehensible to all but herself; but her own perceptions were clear and distinct that in these agonizing throes the most interior and refined elements of her spiritual being were imparted to, and absorbed by, the appropriate portions of the mechanism — its minerals having been made peculiarly receptive by previous chemical processes. This seemed no more absurd or unphilosophical than the well-known fact that a gold ring, or any other article worn about the person, becomes impregnated to a degree with spiritual emanations, or that the elements of one's being can be and are imparted to an autograph so fully that the character, capacities, and may be psychomtrized therefrom.

After the alleged "spiritual birth", Spears and his followers claimed that they could see the machine moving. It continued to make subtle, sporadic movements over the next few weeks. (Specifically, small spheres suspended by wires would occasionally move slightly.)

The *New Era* reported on this as well:

The result of this phenomenon was, that indications of life or pulsation became apparent in the mechanism; first to her own keenly sensitive touch, and soon after to the eyes of all beholders. These pulsations continued to increase, under a process, which she was impelled to continue for some weeks, precisely analogous to that of nursing (for which preparation had previously been made in her own organization, while she was in utter ignorance of any such design), until at times a very marked and surprising motion resulted. At every step in these singular transactions, Mrs. M. has been attended by angelic intelligences (whose presence is perceived by her own interior senses), who have from time to time explained the rationale of their proceedings and of her experiences, and unfolded, in various departments of science, philosophy, and morals, principles and truths of the highest practical moment to us and to mankind. These teachings have been, to a great extent, based upon, and elucidated by, the various experiences connected with that mechanism; and they have been not only profound and comprehensive, intellectually considered, but of the highest, purest, and most elevating moral and spiritual character. That these intelligences have infused into her spirit a most beautiful, harmonizing, celestial influence, has been perceived by all who have enjoyed communication with her, and none of these, I feel assured, will hesitate to endorse the admission that 'she gets a large influx of superior, saving, harmonizing truths.'

The crazy group then bestowed their creation with a number of names, including "Physical Savior," "the New Messiah," "Heaven's Last Best Gift to Man," "The Great Spiritual Revelation of the Age," and "The Philosopher's Stone." The story naturally made waves and even elicited a response from P.T. Barnum, who humorously stated that "If things like this are going to happen, the ladies will be afraid to sleep alone in the house if so much as a sewing-machine or apple-corer be about."

Hopes for the mechanical messiah remained high, and some even speculated that it might be able to "bear offspring" in the form of a race of self-replicating, self-powering machines. This would effectively remedy the "Curse of Adam", or humanity's fate to toil away working the soil, etc. However, within a few weeks, the mechanical marvel forsook its followers. The little movements weren't so exciting anymore and like all cult members coming down from a high, they began to make excuses. Some argued that the spirits possessing the machine weren't heavenly and were simple human ghosts who weren't capable of any truly divine acts.

NEW MOTIVE POWER

SPEARS' STRANGE MACHINE.

Spears decided to take his contraption to Randolph, New York, in hopes that the area would somehow be more conducive in terms of electricity. Just like Dr. Frankenstein, eventually the townsfolk learned of Spears' unholy abomination and broke out the pitchforks and torches. Well, actually I don't know if there were any pitchforks or torches involved, but Spears did claim that an angry mob came to destroy his machine.

In a letter, Spears reported that,

> ...under the cover of the night, the mob entered, tore out the heart of the mechanism, trampled beneath their feet, and scattered it to the four winds. I know the friends who were engaged in constructing this mechanism, and those who cheerfully gave of their means to promote the work, will mourn that the world has not yet arrived at a condition when it could welcome a philanthropic effort of this kind; but thus it is. It did not wish the effort to succeed, and it determined it should not.

The *Scientific American* believed this story was made up, and reported in November of 1854 that,

> We do not believe a word respecting a mob breaking into the building and destroying the spiritual machine. We are of the opinion that it was broken by the crafty author of it, whose schemes had come to the exact point of exposing his ridiculous pretensions.

And indeed, to this day, some do believe that Spears made up the story so that he could hide the machine away somewhere safe. Is there a chance that one day the Anti-Christ or some other, lesser false messiah will come in the form of Spears' infernal machine? That's pretty doubtful, but here's what we do know for sure.

In 1872, Spears claimed his spirit guides in the Association of Electrizers had encouraged him to retire, and so he did. He died fifteen years later in Philadelphia, but that isn't the end of the story. In 2019, the infernal machine was possibly discovered in an attic in Greeley, Colorado, lending credence to the theory that it wasn't really destroyed. The attic belonged to a notorious hoarder nicknamed "Old Lady Crackerman" (real name Miss Akerman). Hoarder may not paint the most flattering picture of Miss Akerman, as she hoarded her belongings in a mansion just outside of town. (In other words, she was a rich hoarder, at least.) When she died, her will stated that she wanted her antique collection sold off to benefit various pet rescues.

On the final week of the clean-up, in the furthest corner of the mansion was found a curious machine with an engraving that read "New Motive Power - John Murray Spear". This being the year 2019, a quick Google search told the discoverers all they needed to know about the odd artifact within minutes.

Inside a drawer of the table portion of the machine was found a picture of Spears, a strange arrow-shaped stone with what looked to be the all-seeing eye on it, and a crucifix among other things. Atop the machine was a tiny, creepy, skull-like head. However, the machine is far from being a dead ringer for the machine in the old engraving, and quite a few people think it was just a fake or reproduction of some sort. That said, it seems odd that someone would go to that much trouble to recreate something as relatively obscure as Spears machine. So, perhaps we should entertain the notion that both the drawings and written descriptions of Spears' machine were inaccurate and possibly the creation in Miss Akerman's attic was the real thing?

Either way, conclusively speaking, the fate and whereabouts of Spears' Infernal Machine are still unknown.

Sources:

Baines, Dan. "John Murray Spear's 'Mechanical Messiah' Discovered in Colorado Attic." (July 03, 2019) http://www.danbaines.com/blog/john-murray-spears-mechanical-messiah-discovered-in-colorado-attic/3/7/2019

Swancer, Brent. "The Strange Case of John Spear and the God Machine." Mysterious Universe (April 24, 2020). https://mysteriousuniverse.org/2020/04/the-strange-case-of-john-spear-and-the-god-machine/

CHAPTER 20
SPRING HEELED JACK STATESIDE

In London, in the late 1830s, there came a strange flap of sightings centering around a being known as Spring Heeled Jack. Naturally, the description differed depending upon the witness, but fundamentally Spring Heeled Jack had the shape and appearance of a man. Sometimes the man was tall and thin, other times stocky and burly. Some reports had him wearing a cape with a lamp on his chest, others claimed he had wings—a few even said that he breathed fire. The common denominator was always that the man-thing could jump significant distances, hence the name Spring Heeled Jack.

For the year of 1837 the police paid no mind to the sightings for the most part. In February of 1838 came forward a respectable citizen who in all earnestness claimed that his daughter had been assaulted by the being. He reported the incident to the police, stating that the previous night his daughter, Jane Alsop, had heard a ring at the gate. Outside, a tall man, shrouded in fog and wearing a cloak, claimed that he was a police officer who had just captured Spring Heeled Jack. The officer asked her to hurry and get a lantern. When she went out to meet the man, he threw off his cloak revealing a "hideous and frightful appearance". He was wearing some sort of helmet and clad in a tight, shiny white suit (she compared it to "white oilskin"). His hands ended in metallic claws, which he reached out to the girl with, tearing her dress in the process. And to top it all off, he breathed blue and white flames! The girl's screams attracted more townsfolk and Jack bounded away into the night as he always did.

A few nights later, a woman named Lucy Sales was walking along a respectable Limehouse street when she was accosted by the same figure along with her sister. Actually, Sales didn't get a good look at the figure because as soon as she saw it, it breathed "a quantity of blue flame" in the direction of her face. The flame blinded her briefly thereafter, and she collapsed to the ground as her sister came to her side, and Jack merely walked away.

A fire-breathing man with metal claws wearing a helmet and a shiny jumpsuit? If this doesn't sound like a B-movie alien, nothing does, and yet it was reported all the way back in 1830s London. Due to this strange appearance, in the 1950s, writers began to speculate that perhaps Jack was an alien of some sort. One went as far as to speculate Jack came from a planet with high gravity, hence his ability to bound through Earth's with ease.

SPRING HEELED JACK.

The theory that Jack was some kind of E.T. is corroborated by way of an 1880 sighting all the way over in Louisville, Kentucky. In July of that year the leaping fiend began being spotted in Old Louisville. Like the other Spring Heeled Jack, this figure was tall, thin, wore a jumpsuit and helmet and had a lamp on his chest. He also tore at several womens' dresses and would perform high leaps and bounds. The creature was reported within the town boundaries (jumping over a horse-drawn carriage no less!) and also outlaying farms where he was seen leaping over a haystack![60]

Around the same time as these sightings took place, the *Louisville Courier-Journal* reported a UFO sighting on July 28, 1880. What made it intriguing was the fact that it was piloted by a man. The article reads,

A FLYING MACHINE

WHAT TWO LOUISVILLIANS SAW LAST EVENING

Between 6 and 7 o'clock last evening while C.A. Youngman and Ben Floxner were standing at a side window of Haddart's drugstore, at Second and Chestnut streets, looking, they discovered an object high up in the air apparently immediately above the Ohio River Bridge, which they at first thought was the wreck of a toy balloon. As it got nearer they observed that it had the appearance of a man surrounded by machinery, which he seemed to be working with his feet and hands. He worked his feet as though he was running a treadle and his arms seem to be swinging to and fro above his head, though the latter movement sometimes appeared to be executed with wings or fans. The gazers became

---

[60] Holland, *Weird Kentucky* p.59.

considerably worked up by the apparition, and inspected it very closely. They could see the delicate outlines of machinery, but the object was too high up to make out its exact construction. At times it would seem to be descending, and then the man appeared to exert himself considerably, and ran the machine faster, when it would ascend again and assume a horizontal position. It did not travel as fast as a paper balloon, and its course seem to be entirely under the control of the aeronaut. At first it was traveling in a southeastward direction, but when it reached a point just over the city, it turned and went due south, until it had passed nearly over the city, when it taxed to the southwest, in which direction it was going when it passed out of sight in the twilight of the evening. The gentleman who saw it are confident that it was a man navigating the air on a flying machine. His movements were regular, and the machine was under the most perfect control. If he belongs to this mundane sphere he should have dropped his card as he passed over, to enlighten those who saw him, and that his friends, if he has any, might be informed of his whereabouts.

Though the witnesses didn't really describe the man within the sphere, it seems too much a coincidence that the sphere showed up at the same time as the mysterious spring-heeled visitor. As for the craft itself, it sounded a bit like an autogiro, a relatively small helicopter-like craft that had yet to be invented.

ANOTHER PERIOD SPRING HEELED JACK ILLUSTRATION.

Only an hour or two later, a second sighting was recorded in Madisonville, Kentucky. There a family observed a "circular form" that changed into an "oval". It also had "a ball at each end of the thing". The relevant portion of the article goes as follows:

THE FLYING MACHINE

Another witness of reliability to the Courier-Journal's aerial navigator who has solved the problem.

Dr. DS Dempsey, of Madisonville, Kentucky., Has written the following to the Madisonville times concerning the flying machine which was observed passing over the city two weeks ago:

"I interviewed Mr. Wells, the proprietor of the marble shop, N. Main St., and Mr. Royster, a workman in said shop, in regard to what he and his family saw hop over Madisonville last Wednesday, but was not positive as to the day. Mr. Wells stated that Mr. Royster told him about it the day that an account of a flying machine over Louisville was published in the Courier-Journal. I asked them both, particularly Mr. Wells, was it before we received the Courier-Journal. This reply was in emphatic that it was in the morning of the day we received said Courier-Journal. Mr. Royster stated that the evening before, which would be Wednesday, between sundown and dark, his son Johnny, six or seven years old, called his attention to something he saw hopping over Madisonville.

He, Mr. Royster, and his wife and other children went out and looked at it. They live in southeastern Madisonville, about half mile from the railroad depot. He said there seem to be a ball at each end of the thing, and it looked as if it was about over the depot. It sometimes appeared in a circular form and changed it to an oval. It passed out of sight going, as well as he could determine, directly south. Everybody knows Mr. Wells and will believe that what he said in regard to the time Mr. Royster told him these things is strictly true.

The article goes on to speculate that perhaps men will soon travel through the air themselves. It then dovetails into a humorous ending with a political joke. "No one will suppose that the gentleman who flew over Louisville and Madisonville was Gabriel, for he did not toot his horn; but someone suggests that the gentleman in the aerial chariot was the devil himself sent down by the Republicans to the south in behalf of their sinking ship."

It is possible that Spring Heeled Jack, or an entity of the same species, had been in America for some time now. During the Civil War on the battlefield of Gettysburg, Pennsylvania, in July of 1863 was seen a strange 'Spring-heeled' being 'flittering' around the dead. The man-thing was described as being tall with glowing green eyes and wearing a dark cape or cloak of some kind. Four years later, Jack made what might have been his first appearance in Kentucky at Mount Sterling on

November 6, 1868. About thirty people sighted the man-thing perched atop the Old Farmers Bank building. They also saw it circling around the Gaitskell Indian Burial Mound. (If they meant circling on the ground, or circling in the air, isn't clear.)

The 1880 Kentucky sighting wasn't the last time Jack was seen in America. In May of 1905, the spring-heeled specter came to Philadelphia, Pennsylvania. A woman named Julia McGlone was leaving work when a figure leaped down and attacked her with sharp claws. The woman screamed, drawing the attention of a policeman who ran to her rescue. In typical Jack fashion, the being blew blue flames at the man's face and then flew up a flight of stairs in a single bound! As usual, this being was wearing metallic-looking clothing.

The 1930s saw a resurgence of U.S.-based Jack sightings. Again in Kentucky, this time in Ashland, a winged humanoid was seen flitting through the sky in March 1938.[61] In April of that same year, Elizabethtown, Kentucky, reported similar sightings. That summer, Spring Heeled Jack was even seen in Silver City, New Mexico, of all places!

A 1980 letter to the Center for UFO Studies related the sighting:

We all saw him. He was dressed all in gray and he even seemed gray; he was drifting or floating at tree-top level. The thing I remember the most about him was that he seemed to be wearing a

---

[61] Though it could also have been Mothman.

belt which was wide and had points sticking out of it. He also seemed to be wearing a cape (a la Flash Gordon).

He drifted across the sky above us and we all stood and stared, speechless. It did not occur to us to question this phenomena [sic]; as children we accepted it....

About fifteen years ago I was telling my husband about it. When I did, I questioned myself—perhaps I had had a dream. But just in case, I called my brother. By now I was about thirty-five and he about thirty-two. I prefaced my conversation by telling him that I had a strange story to tell and that perhaps it had all been a dream, but that I thought that in about 1938 I had seen a man fly over our heads. He stopped me and said, "It wasn't a dream." He went on to describe everything as I have described it here, including the belt and the cape.[62]

Ultimately, we can only wonder if these creatures were the same being seen in London, or if not the same being, one of the same species.

Sources:

Clark, Jerome. *The Unexplained.* Visible Ink Press, 1998.

Holland, Jeffrey Scott. *Weird Kentucky.* Union Square & Co., 2008.

---

[62] Clark, *The Unexplained*, Kindle Edition.

CHAPTER 21
BILLY THE KIDS
RESTLESS BONES

No outlaw's life after death can compete with that of William H. Bonney, alias Billy the Kid. While it's true that both Butch Cassidy and Jesse James were said to escape death's clutches—at least as far as the accepted historical record goes—Billy the Kid's life after death is truly unequaled. Not only did he have nearly a dozen men claiming to be him after his death in 1881, but his grave markers have also been stolen nearly a half dozen times as well!

Much of what is known of the Kid can be attributed to legend over fact, including his birthdate of November 23, 1859 (which is also conveniently the birthday of his first biographer, Ash Upson). The Kid led a rough life, losing his mother in Silver City, New Mexico, to tuberculosis at the age of fifteen in 1874. After that began his life of what some call crime and others just call survival in the Wild West. He was forced to kill a man in self defense in Arizona and migrated back to New Mexico not long after. There he found himself embroiled in the bloody Lincoln County range war of 1878. After this, Billy relied on rustling cattle to get by and was gunned down by Sheriff Pat Garrett in Fort Sumner in July of 1881... allegedly.

Tall tales exist that either Garrett shot the wrong man or conspired with the Kid to let him escape, but we won't go down that rabbit hole here. Besides, firmer evidence seems to suggest that the

THE DEVIL COMES FOR BILLY

THE FINALE—THE KID KILLED BY THE SHERIFF AT FORT SUMNER. Page 128.

Billy's obituaries which ran in papers as far away as London were fairytale like, the most obscene belonging to the Santa Fe *Weekly Democrat* which reported after the Kid hit the floor dead, a strong odor of brimstone filled the room. Accompanying the brimstone was the very devil himself to take Billy's soul, or at least according to the *Weekly Democrat.*

Kid was laid to rest in the Old Fort Sumner Cemetery. However, I use the term rest loosely, for only a year after being planted in the ground, his grave marker, a crude wooden cross made of fenceposts, was stolen by his ex-girlfriend, Paulita Maxwell.

**THE KID'S FOOTSTONE RETURNED TO
FORT SUMNER.**

Paulita and her brother Pete had a $10 wager going that she would be too afraid to go out to Billy's grave at midnight due to Billy's ghost. When Paulita agreed to make the short journey to the cemetery, Pete insisted that she bring back a weed or flower to prove she had been there, only she brought back the entire cross to her doubting brother. The next morning Paulita sent one of the servants to put the cross back into the ground. As it turned out, Paulita begat a tradition of stealing Billy's marker. Years later, the crude wooden cross would be stolen away to New England. When it was replaced many years later by a nice footstone, it was

203

stolen in 1950 and not recovered until 1976! It was stolen again in 1981 and recovered within a week. After that, the footstone was literally shackled to the gravesite, and a jail cell was built around the burial plot.

BILLY THE KID, THE BOY BANDIT KING.

VAMPIRES, MUMMIES, AND WEREWOLVES
OF THE WILD WEST

More macabre than the theft of Billy's markers is the alleged theft of his bones themselves. The first story regarding the mutilation of the Kid's body appeared in the July 25, 1881, edition of the *Las Vegas Optic* in their now infamous "The Fatal Finger" story:

> An esteemed friend of the *Optic* at Fort Sumner, L.W. Hale, has sent us the index finger of "Billy, the Kid," the one which has snapped many a man's life into eternity. It is well preserved in alcohol and has been viewed by many in our office today. If the rush continues we shall purchase a small tent and open a side show to which complementary tickets will be issued to our personal friends.[63]

Though for many years this story was thought to be a hoax, professor emeritus Robert J. Stahl wrote a lengthy piece on the trigger finger for *True West* magazine. Stahl clarified that people actually did trek to the *Optic* office to see a finger in a jar. Whether it was really Billy's or not is unknown, but reportedly they were allowed to gaze upon it so long as they paid $3 for a yearlong subscription to the paper!

As it turned out, the mysterious donor, L.W. Hale, was a real New Mexico resident and a first class peddler. A relative once said of him, "He was a wheeler and dealer, but always an honest and fair

---

[63] *Billy the Kid: Las Vegas Newspaper Accounts Of His Career, 1880-1881.*

wheeler and dealer."[64] The family also confirmed Hale was indeed in the Ft. Sumner area at the time of the Kid's death and was a friend of *Optic* editor Russell A. Kistler.

An even more macabre story appeared in the *Optic* on September 10th entitled "The Kid Kidnapped" and read:

The fifth day after the burial of the notorious young desperado, a fearless skelologist of this county, whose name, for substantial reasons, cannot be divulged, proceeded to Sumner, and in the silent watches of the night, with the assistance of a compadre, dug up the remains of the once mighty youth and carried them off in their wagon. The "stiff" was brought in to Las Vegas, arriving here at two o'clock in the morning, and was slipped quietly into the private office of a practical "sawbones," who, by dint of diligent labor and careful watching to prevent detection, boiled and scraped the skin off the "plate" so as to secure the skull, which was seen by a reporter last evening. The body, or remains proper, was covered in dirt in the corral, where it will remain until decomposition shall have robbed the frame of its meat, when the body will be dug up again and the skeleton "fixed up"—hung together by wires and varnished with shellac to make it presentable. Then the physicians will feel that their labors

---

[64] Stahl, "Lower William Hale and Joshua Fred Hale," *Lincoln County, New Mexico Tells its Tales.*

have been rewarded, for the skeleton of a crack frontiersman does not grow on every bush, and the "bones" of such men as the Kid are hard to find. The skull is already "dressed," and is considered quite a relic in itself. The index finger of the right hand, it will be remembered, was presented to THE OPTIC at the time the exhumation was made. As this member has been sent east, the skeleton now in process of consummation will not be complete in its fingers; but the loss is so trivial that it will be hardly noticeable.

According to Ft. Sumner resident Charles Foor, these newspaper articles caught the attention of Pat Garrett. A 1928 article in the *Southwestern Dispatch* related that "Mr. For [sic] said that he had inspected the grave in the company of Pat Garrett 18 months after the internment and when the first claim of the moving of the bones was made by the Las Vegas people. At that time both men agreed that the grave was untouched."

One of Garrett's biographers, Richard O'Connor, claimed that Garret visited the grave several weeks later after his "indignation was aroused by reports that carnivals, dime museums, and other opportunistic enterprises were displaying what they claimed where parts of Billy's corpse." O'Connor also claimed that Garrett even dug up the body to make sure, but this is doubtful. Whatever the case, Garrett addressed the rumors in his book *Authentic Life of Billy the Kid.*

PAT GARRETT.

I said that the body was buried in the cemetery at Ft. Sumner. I wish to add that it is there today intact—skull, fingers, toes, bones, and every hair on the head that was buried with the body on that 15th of July, doctors, newspaper editors, and paragraphers to the contrary now withstanding. Some presuming swindlers have claimed to have the Kid's skull on exhibition, or one of his fingers, or some other portion of his body, and one medical gentleman has persuaded credulous idiots that he has all the bones strung up on wires...Again I say the Kid's body lies undisturbed in the grave—and I speak of what I know.

VAMPIRES, MUMMIES, AND WEREWOLVES
OF THE WILD WEST

The saga of Billy's body parts continued on September 19, when the *Optic* received a letter from a woman, Kate Tenney of Oakland, California, alleging to be the Kid's ex-lover requesting that she be given the notorious trigger finger. The editor then replied to the woman that it had already been sold for $150. The editor went on to joke that perhaps the sawbones who had Billy's corpse from the September 10th story could send the poor girl "a shank bone—or something of that kind." While the *Optic* editor, Russell Kistler, is usually attributed to cooking up the letter, this story was actually run by another editor at the *Optic*, Lute Wilcox. The finger was supposedly sold to one Albert Kunz, who operated a drug store in Las Vegas. Kistler wrote of Kunz's departure to Waterville, Kansas, and indeed the *Waterville Telegraph* reported on September 16th that "Mr. Albert Kunz returned home last Monday from Las Vegas. He is looking hale and hearty, and brought as a relic of barbarism a specimen of the physical existence of Billy the Kid."[65]

The *Optic* kept up its coverage of Billy's traveling finger in their October 14th issue, where it was reported that it was now on display in Indiana at several county fairs. This was the last item to be reported on the finger's whereabouts, and it is presumed to be lost. Thanks to the 'Fatal Finger' story, readership to the *Optic* soared, so other

---

[65] Stahl, "The Mysterious Journey of Billy the Kid's Trigger Finger," *True West*.

newspapers began to follow suit. In 1885 the *Silver City Enterprise* wrote a story on the Kid's skull being in the possession of an Albuquerque man.

Billy the Kid's Grave, as it appears in 1928, and his two pals' graves on each side of him. Photo by A. M. Sparks, Winters, Texas.

**THE KID'S GRAVE C.1928
WHEN IT WAS UNMARKED.**

Despite those claims, most likely Billy's bones still rest under the Fort Sumner ground, as evidenced by a few sightings of the Kid's ghost. Of the old cemetery, Charlie Foor said in Walter Noble Burns' *Saga of Billy the Kid* that "They say it's haunted. Some folks'll drive a mile out of their way at night to keep from passin' it." Burns gave a characteristic vivid description of the Kid's grave, then a barren patch of land devoid of a proper marker:

The bare space is perhaps the length of a man's body. Salt grass grows in a mat all around it, but queerly enough stops short at the edges and not a blade sprouts upon it. A Spanish gourd vine with ghostly gray pointed leaves stretches its trailing length toward the blighted spot but, within a few inches of its margin, veers sharply off to one side as if with conscious purpose to avoid contagion. Perfectly bare the space is except for a shoot of prickly pear that crawls across it like a green snake; a gnarled bristly, heat cursed desert cactus crawling like a snake across the heart of Billy the Kid. "It's always bare like this," says Old Man Foor, standing back from this spot as if half-afraid of some inexplicable contamination. "I don't know why. Grass or nothin' else will grow on it—that's all. You might almost think there's poison in the ground."

Foor even suggested that cracks in the hard dry earth made out the picture of a skeletal hand reaching out from certain angles. Burns went on to concur, perhaps merely for the delight of his readers, that he too saw "the sun-drawn skiagraph" that somehow stretched from the grave.

Saga also included a brief comical episode on the Maxwell family involving the Kid's ghost shortly after his death in the chapter "The Belle of Old Fort Sumner." One night Paulita and Pete Maxwell with a neighbor, Manuel Abreu, were sitting inside when they heard the sound of soft footsteps walking across the front porch as if someone were creeping along in their stalking feet. "Can it be that the Kid has come back from the dead?" an excited Abreu asked. Pete Maxwell chimed in and remarked, "Every night since his death I've heard queer noises about the old house." Paulita was the voice of reason among the men, who were perhaps just trying to scare her, and chided them for their foolishness. "But Paulita, they say the spirits of murdered men return to haunt the place where they were killed," Abreu continued. The footsteps began again and Maxwell crossed himself, "Billy the Kid's ghost!" Finally having enough, Paulita went outside to investigate only to find it was merely a jackrabbit. It is reported in other stories that Pete really did fear the ghost of Billy, for when it came time to sell his ranch a short time later to the New England Cattle Company, Maxwell insisted he could not sell Billy's favorite horse, Don, or "Billy, dead these three years, would rise up in his grave and curse me."[66] Likewise, Deluvina Maxwell, a

---

[66] Kadlec, *They "Knew" Billy the Kid*, 122.

close friend of the Kid's, was herself wildly
superstitious and would not pass the cemetery after
dark, claiming to have seen the ghost of a buffalo
soldier there once, but never Billy.

THE OLD BILLY THE KID CURIO SHOP.

An old *True West* article by artist Lea F.
McCarty relating his trek to Fort Sumner to find a
picture of the Kid's funeral mentions tales of Billy's
ghost several times but fails to go into detail on
them. The closest the article gets to a bonafide Billy
ghost sighting comes from a conversation between
McCarty and Tom Sullivan, a clerk at the Billy the
Kid Curio Shop near the grave. McCarty asked
why the property owner never sold the cemetery to
the state, to which Sullivan replied, "They don't
want it." He then leaned in close to elaborate:

He bent over to whisper with the wind howling
outside..."Some say [the owner] is afeard of
Billy's ghost. It's been seen, you know, by some

of the folks around here. Mr. Austin saw it, so he says, riding one night across the old fort ruins and carrying the wooden cross. He rode the beautiful grey he was so proud of. *Duerme bien querido.*"

The Spanish phrase whispered by Sullivan at the end was the inscription "Rest in peace, beloved" said to be on the original cross. When Sullivan went on to recount the poor long gone cross's elaborate history, he mentioned how Paulita Maxwell once stole it to win a bet. "That wouldn't have been me sir! I've seen Billy's ghost myself, but I don't expect you to believe it!"

Sources:

Carson, Kit. "Billy the Kid's Restless Bones." *Real West* (March 1962).

Kadlec, Robert F. Ed. *They "Knew" Billy the Kid.* Ancient City Press, 1987.

McCarty, Lea F. "Why is it so important that theirs is a photograph of Billy the Kid's Funeral?" *True West* (November-December 1960)

Morrison, William. *Billy the Kid: Las Vegas Newspaper Accounts Of His Career, 1880-1881.* W. M. Morrison-Books, 1958.

Stahl, Robert J. "The Mysterious Journey of Billy the Kid's Trigger Finger." *True West* (July 2013).

CHAPTER 22
VAMPIRE CHAIR OF TENNESSEE

The following tale begins very appropriately with the discovery of a dead body buried at a crossroads. And not just any random dead body. It was buried facedown, had been partially mummified from minerals in the ground, and most important of all, it had a stake driven through its heart.

The year was 1917 and the body was found near Oostanaula Creek in Bradley County, Tennessee, not far from Charleston. It was discovered by a road crew working to widen a road that curved around a river bluff. Those familiar with legends of the Crossroads Demon will no doubt find it interesting that the body was discovered at a crossroads itself. As stated before, it was petrified, and this being the year 1917, that meant it had been buried at some point the previous century.

As the workers examined the body, they discovered the wooden stake through the heart. Nor was it a stake carved for that purpose. Ever seen a vampire movie where the hero grabs a fencepost or a broken chair leg to impale the vampire? That's apparently what happened here, as the men were able to determine that it was indeed a chair leg and not a petrified piece of wood.

They were able to tell because it wasn't just any old chair leg, but a very ornate one that must've come from a wealthy home. Back then, chairs were a big deal, as they signified one's financial well-standing depending on how nice they were. The workmen recognized the chair leg as the work of Eli and Jacob Odom, a couple of early day Tennessee settlers renowned for their distinctive chair designs, notably the "mule-eared chair."

Local lore referred to the corpse as "the woman from Hiwassee" and "the witch lady". Some think that her name was remembered but locals were too fearful to utter it out loud. This wasn't unique to Tennessee, and many cultures attribute a certain power or taboo to speaking a powerful name aloud. Native Americans don't like to utter the names of witches or skinwalkers as they fear that it will draw them near. So, that the Appalachian peoples were fearful of uttering the alleged witch's name wasn't out of left field.

Oral tradition says that in life the witch woman had the stereotypical appearance of a witch as an old hag with dry skin reminiscent of a snake and mouth that emitted foul breath. Naturally, she lived in a lonely cabin on the bluff and rarely ventured out unless she had to buy supplies. Animals seemed to fear her, and birds shied away from her cabin. The people of the area shunned her publicly but were said to visit her in secret when her services were desired.

She used local plant life to create powerful potions to either cure ailments or induce them. She could also make love potions and she was said to have attributes of what we would call the skinwalker in the Southwest, being able to transform into a bird, specifically a crow.

Of course, witches were usually burned at the stake or drowned, so why the stake in the heart? That's because, allegedly, she also drank blood. (It apparently didn't do her haggard appearance any favors.) The locals whispered that she would sneak into men's homes as they slept and feed on them. Some said she gained ingress into the house in the form of a black rat, and in that form, she would feed on small children. Others even claimed they had seen her transform into a big black bird on her way to and from victims' homes. However, some have theorized that the woman probably never actually sank her fangs into anyone's neck, and in truth, she used blood in her rituals and potions, and from that the vampire aspect of the story took root.

It is said that the vampire witch's end came about due to an epidemic sweeping the area. Back in those days, vampires and witches were often associated with plagues and illnesses. When a particularly virulent one hit the Charleston area sometime in the early to mid-1800s, it is said that area residents began to blame the old witch up on the bluff. The perennial angry mob of the old Universal monster movies then descended on the witch's cabin and dragged her from it to her death.

In the book, *The Granny Curse and Other Ghosts and Legends from East Tennessee*, an old quote from the *Tennessee Folklore Society Bulletin* pertaining to the land the witch supposedly lived on was reprinted. The land had been owned by the family of the now deceased Frank G. Trewhitt, who stated, "The land on which the body was found belonged to my great-grandfather and was passed to his sons. If they ever had heard any vampire tales hereabouts, I would have been told."

For those wondering if there might be some other, more logical explanation for a woman found buried at a crossroads with a stake through her heart, there really are none. Let's say a woman did suffer a freak accident where she had a chair leg impaled in her chest, it's unlikely she would have been buried in the middle of nowhere. (Unless, perhaps, she was murdered for some reason.)

Wooden stakes aside, it's also important to note that the woman was buried facedown. In the "Old Country" (i.e. Eastern Europe) burying a vampire facedown was a common custom and served as a way of ensuring that it didn't dig its way back to the surface, the thought process being that when it began to claw its way through the dirt, it would dig itself deeper and deeper into the earth. They were also buried at crossroads because it was thought that if they emerged, the intersection may confuse them and they would not know which way to go. Plus, the frequent passing of horses and wagons would keep the ground packed firmly in place. Anyhow, while we can't prove that the corpse found along the crossroads in 1917 really was a vampire, it's certainly obvious that whoever killed the woman believed she was.

ORNATE ANTIQUE CHAIR.

But the story still doesn't end there. Believe it or not, a legend is also attached to the chair that the leg was broken off of to impale the witch! And, actually, this legend might just be more interesting than the story of the witch itself.

According to lore, and in spite of what you might expect, the villagers didn't burn the witch's abode down after they were done with her. Sensible folk, they instead ransacked the house and divided her more valuable belongings amongst themselves, including the Odom chair with the leg broken off. The chair was repaired and taken to someone's residence. But, the occupants soon noticed that the chair itself had become a vampire! That's right, a vampire chair. Supposedly, the chair felt comfortable at first until suddenly, inexplicably, the sitter suddenly feels stuck to the chair, as if they are being drained of their energy and cannot stand. Eventually, a scratch would appear on either the forearm or the leg, and a small drop of blood would fall to the floor under the chair. After that, the occupant could finally stand and escaped the cursed chair.

Naturally, someone eventually got the idea to destroy the chair, but how does one stake a piece of vampire furniture made of wood? Supposedly, when residents went to destroy it, it was supernaturally impervious to their blows and so they gave it away. Other stories said that residents were actually too frightened to destroy the chair and never even tried for fear of another curse falling upon them, and so they simply set it in an abandoned area for some other poor soul to come along and collect it.

The chair made the rounds and was allegedly last seen at various locations across Tennessee, either on the porch a hotel near Charleston, an old house in Greeneville, at an antiques shop in Kingsport and so on. Others whisper it has traveled out of state, and maybe even out of the country to Europe, where the old witch woman's spirit still haunts it. But, just in case the Europe story isn't true, be wary of antique chairs in Tennessee...

Sources:

Curran, Bob. *American Vampires: Their True Bloody History From New York to California.* Weiser, 2012.

Russel, Randy and Janet Barnett. *The Granny Curse and Other Ghosts and Legends from East Tennessee.* Blair, 1999.

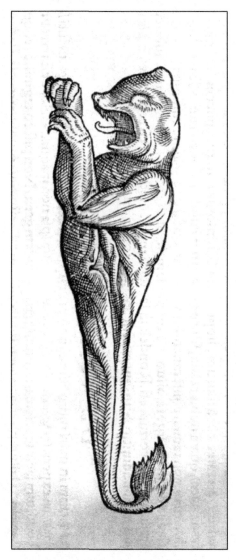

GESNER'S *SIMIA MARINA*,
OR SEA MONKEY.

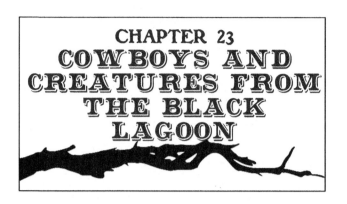

CHAPTER 23
COWBOYS AND CREATURES FROM THE BLACK LAGOON

On August 22, 1972, an article out of Thetis Lake in British Columbia reported the impossible: two teenage boys had seen a real-life Gillman. The boys described the creature as having "silvery scaled skin, sharp claws, and spikes on its head."

Mike Gold, one of the boys, went on to say that the monster "was shaped like an ordinary body, like a human being body but it had a monster face and it was all scaly." It also had "great big ears," so while not a dead ringer for the Gillman from *Creature from the Black Lagoon* (1954), it was close.

22

Years later Daniel Loxton, editor of *Skeptic* magazine, was smart enough to figure out that something truly was fishy about this story and it wasn't just the monster. The week preceding the sighting a local television station had aired a rip-off of *Creature from the Black Lagoon*. The film was 1965's *Monster from the Surf*, and featured a monster matching the Thetis Lake creature's exact description—pointy head and all. To drive the final nail into the proverbial coffin, Loxton even re-interviewed one of the witnesses and got them to admit that the story was completely made up (and inspired by *Monster from the Surf*).

This, unfortunately, put a real dampener on real-life gillmen sightings. However, gillmen and fish-people had been reported in newspapers for years and years... long before the invention of motion pictures. In fact, the Gillman himself of *Creature from the Black Lagoon* (1954) was inspired by a real Amazonian legend.[67] What follows is a menagerie of articles and news items on close contenders for a real "Creature from the Black Lagoon" sighted during America's early days.

Not to be confused with Stellar's Sea Ape sighting off the coast of Alaska in 1741, off the coast of Southern California was sighted a humanoid sea monster in 1823. A traveler by the name of Hernando Grijalva was the lucky witness who spotted something he described as half-monkey, half fish. However, unlike Stellar's better-known Sea Ape, which was limbless, this creature had

---

[67] See *Cowboys & Saurians South of the Border* for that story.

human-like arms. The head was described as dog-like and the torso as that of a woman's with a long fish-like tail that divided at the end like a Swallow's. The tail appeared to have scales, and the body was colored like a porpoise. The size of the creature, which could leap out of the water and swim with ease, was said to be in the range of a sea otter.

While that creature sounded more like a grotesque mermaid, the following fish monster from 1888 is more in line with a typical gillman. It was reported in the *Philadelphia Times* of September 9, 1888, on page four:

The Paupack Creek, in Pike County [Pennsylvania], is the dwelling-place of a monster more wonderful than the sea-serpent, if one can believe the stories told by people in the vicinity. They describe the beast as having a head like an ape and square shoulders like a human being. From the shoulders of the creature there extend legs, or arms, which terminate in great claws. The body or the monster, which is fully six feet in length, is of a reddish-brown tint, very like that of a lizard, and terminates in a tail like that of a fish. The creature's body is bare of any covering, but about the head and neck is a mane of reddish hair. It is needless to say that the county is excited over the strange animal. Various parties surround the creek each day, in hopes of capturing the beast, but up to the present time their endeavors have not been crowned with success.

THE IPUPIARA OF SOUTH AMERICA.

The monster was apparently just a one-off, though, as I found no further mention of it. The next article shows that long before the Montauk Monster of 2008, strange things were washing up on the shores of New York State. In this case, the mystery carcass washed up on the shores of Lake Ontario in the town of Wilson, New York. It was reported on page three of the *Wellsville Allegany County Reporter* on July 12, 1901:

A STRANGE ANIMAL
Wilson has a mystery which is puzzling residents

Wilson, July 8. – Residents of this village recently are greatly puzzled over the classification of a strange animal that lies on the beach of Lake Ontario, three miles west of Wilson.

The head is gone but the shoulders and heavyset arms bear a striking resemblance to a human being. The shoulders are broad and the arms are heavy with fingers and claws on the ends of them. The body tapers down like a large fish, but has no fins and is covered with a rough coded skin. It would probably weigh 150 to 200 pounds. The arms are 18 inches long and the body 5 ½ feet long.

And here's another from New Jersey that same year, in December. The article was published in the *Philadelphia Inquirer* on December 22, 1901:

**Strange Animal Loomed Up in Front of a Sea Isle Carpenter and Gave Him a Chase
Special to The Inquirer.**

SEA ISLE CITY, N. J., Dec. 21.—Elmer Peterson, a young carpenter, had an encounter a few nights ago out on the meadow which he will long remember. He was near the thoroughfare in search of ducks and when returning home a large, dark form rose up from the meadow in front of him.

Peterson declares it was not a human being, but some strange animal. It chased him quite a distance, uttering all the while a peculiar, growling sound. He out footed the mysterious beast, which disappeared in the darkness.

Next comes this armless oddity out of Pennsylvania in 1905. The blurb was published in the *Pennsylvania Patriot* on October 23, 1905.

People residing along the river midway between Cly and Goldsboro are mystified and some are alarmed over the sight of a strange creature that has its abode in the Susquehanna River. Two men and their wives have seen the "thing." As it was seen in broad daylight more credence is given to the story than would be had it been seen at night, when people are more prone to see "things." This creature, whether fish or animal, is described as being as large as a man. When seen it came up out of the water erect like a man walking and is described as looking like a man without arms. Those persons who have seen it declare that they are not the victims of an optical illusion.

Rounding out our trip into the realm of the Gillman is this report from Clear Lake, Iowa. Like the others, this one was a one-off with no repeat performances. The article was published in the *Evening Times-Republican* on June 29, 1914:

CLEAR LAKE MYSTERY.

STRANGE INHABITANT OF SHORE WATERS STEALING FOOD NIGHTLY.

CAN'T EXPLAIN PRESENCE OF HUMAN APPEARING FISH.

Appears from Waters of Lake and Steals Food from Wharves May Be Demented Man Who Prefers to Hide and Swim in Lake - Night Vigil of Resorters Fails to Solve Mystery.

Clear Lake, June 29. - What has been termed by the summer colony as the "Human Fish" has been discovered on the north shore of Clear Lake and is causing more excitement than has prevailed at this summer resort for a number of years. The discovery of the strange phenomenon was brought about by cottagers who had food taken off their piers which run into the lake and the statement of a number who declare they have seen the strange creature. Several parties have gone out in an effort to catch the mysterious visitor, but each effort has been, up to date, without result.

A few nights ago, a party of guests at the Oaks Hotel went down to the lake beach and started in an all-night vigil in an effort to capture it. Just at midnight when the lights went out about the pier, a ripple in the water was seen and a human arm was extended out of the water. It grabbed some food which had been placed on the end of the pier and was again withdrawn into the water. The watchers rushed to the pier end, but they saw nothing. However, a dark spot a ways out in the lake near 100 yards away was seen hurrying thru the water and a weird laugh was heard rippling over the water.

Some fishermen who were out in a boat last Thursday claim to have seen what they took to be a man swimming with fish-like speed thru the water. They gave chase in their boat but as they neared the man or animal, it dove, and a similar laughter was heard from the rushes which were about fifty yards away.

Sea Monster or Man?

It is believed that the strange inhabitant of the lake, is either a sea monster which has by some method found a home in the lake or else it is a demented man whose love for swimming has caused him to spend most of his time in the water, getting his food from the piers and cottages and sleeping like Moses of old, in the bull rushes along the lake's shore. The proximity of the county home between Clear Lake and Mason City where a number of unfortunates are housed, led to an investigation and it was found that there are none of the inmates missing. Instead of solving the mystery the solutions seemed farther away.

Hunting the human fish has become a pastime with the colonists. The description given by those who claimed to have seen it describe it as a small sized man about 50 years of age and whose body seems to be covered with scales like a fish, caused perhaps by the roughening of his skin by constant staving in the water. Others claim it is impossible for the creature to be a man because of the long time it stays under water. However, every effort is being made to solve the mystery and motor launch loads of people can be seen daily skirting the lake looking for the strange creature whose mysterious visits have so aroused the summer colony.

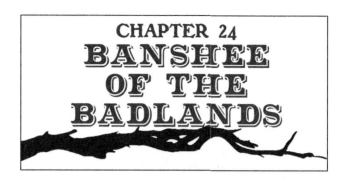

CHAPTER 24
BANSHEE OF THE BADLANDS

The legend of the Banshee, or the woman of the fairy mound, is an Irish one. The banshee is notorious for its shrieking and wailing, and glimpsing one is thought to herald or precede the death of a family member. Wraith-like in appearance, the banshee usually has long hair and a dress that flails in the wind as she screams.

In North America, one of the best-known places to sight a banshee is the Badlands of South Dakota. It's an appropriate spot for a spook, with its craggy rock spires and canyon mazes. In 1864, General Alfred Sully aptly described the Badlands as "Hell with the fire gone out."

BADLANDS SOUTH DAKOTA

In *Myths and Legends of Our Own Lands,*
Charles M. Skinner wrote of the Banshee of the
Badlands:

It may have been the white victim of a red man's
jealousy that haunts the region of the butte
called "Watch Dog," or it may have been an
Indian woman who was killed there, but there is
a banshee in the desert whose cries have chilled
the blood that would not have cooled at the sight
of a bear or panther. By moonlight, when the
scenery is most suggestive and unearthly, and
the noises of wolves and owls inspire uneasy
feelings, the ghost is seen on a hill a mile south
of the Watch Dog, her hair blowing, her arms
tossing in strange gestures.

If war parties, emigrants, cowboys, hunters,
any who for good or ill are going through this
country, pass the haunted butte at night, the

rocks are lighted with phosphor flashes and the banshee sweeps upon them. As if wishing to speak, or as if waiting a question that it has occurred to none to ask, she stands beside them in an attitude of appeal, what if asked what she wants she flings her arms aloft and with a shriek that echoes through the blasted gulches for a mile she disappears and an instant later is seen wringing her hands on her hilltop. Cattle will not graze near the haunted butte and the cowboys keep aloof from it, for the word has never been spoken that will solve the mystery of the region or quiet the unhappy banshee.

The creature has a companion, sometimes, in an unfleshed skeleton that trudges about the ash and clay and haunts the camps in a search for music. If he hears that he will sit outside the door and nod in time to it, while a violin left within his reach is eagerly seized and will be played on through half the night. The music is wondrous: now as soft as the stirrer of wind in the sage, anon as harsh as the cry of a wolf or startling as the stir of a rattler. As the east begins to brighten the music grows fainter, and when it is fairly light it has ceased altogether. But he who listens to it must on no account follow the player if the skeleton moves away, for not only will it lead him into rocky pitfalls, whence escape is hopeless, but when there the music will intoxicate, madden, and will finally charm his soul from his body.[68]

---

[68] Skinner, *Myths and Legends of Our Own Land*, pp.184-185.

COWBOYS & MONSTERS

BANSHEE ILLUSTRATION FROM IRELAND.

To this day, the legend of the Banshee of the Badlands and her skeletal sidekick hasn't been forgotten, and it's still debated who the woman was who lost her life to become the banshee.

A common Banshee of the Badlands folktale will usually go like this: Three cowboys sitting around a campfire on a moonlit night will be having a good time, perhaps telling stories or singing songs. According to the myth, you know what that means—the skeleton man will soon arrive. But before the skeleton man, the men will hear the banshee's fierce cry in the darkness.

The cowboys turn their heads in the direction of Watchdog Butte, and there will see the form of a translucent, blue woman. When not screaming, she might even look beautiful, but when she screams, her eyes turn to black pits of nothingness.

254—"Hell's Half Acre" in the Bad Lands, So. Dak.

Next comes the sound of sweet music as the fiddling skeleton man approaches. As the cowboys become distracted by the music and the sight of the new specter, the banshee fades away. The music soon lulls the cowboys to sleep, and when they awaken in the morning, one of them will be missing. They follow the tracks of their missing companion to a cliffside where he apparently jumped. As they scan the bottom of the cliff, they don't see the dead body of their companion, but a bleached skeleton clutching a fiddle.

Of course, there's never been a version of this story where the cowboys are named, and especially not a version where a death can be confirmed and attributed to the legend of the banshee.

Sources:

Skinner, Charles M. *Myths and Legends of Our Own Land.* J.B. Lippincott Company, 1896.

ISABELLA BURT'S GRAVE.

CHAPTER 25
WEREWOLF
WOMAN OF
TALBOT COUNTY

eorgia's best known werewolf tale is likely that of the poor "werewolf girl" of Talbot County,[69] Isabella Burt. While it can be proven that Burt was indeed a real woman who was born in the 1840s and lived in the area with her mother and three sisters, it's uncertain whether the tales of her werewolf-like deeds are the truth or gross exaggerations.

Variations of the story attest that Isabella didn't begin to resemble a werewolf until after coming home from a trip to Europe, while others state that Isabella inherited her wolf-like looks from her late

---

[69] An odd coincidence in terms of the name, I know, since Lon Chaney Jr.'s character was named Larry Talbot in *The Wolf Man*. However, the county, created in 1827, was named for the deceased Georgia governor Matthew Talbot.

 father. But, as you can see in the picture, the real Isabella wasn't all that wolfish looking. However, Isabella isn't smiling in this picture, either, and if lore is to be believed, her most distinctive feature was her sharp, animal-like teeth. In *Georgia Ghosts*, Nancy Roberts described the girl's teeth as looking like they had been "shaped with a file" and were "pointed." Supposedly, the teeth were so noticeable and distracting that the wealthy Mrs. Burt consulted a dentist as to whether or not anything could be done for her daughter's frightening teeth. However, the dentist said that nothing could be done for the girl's unfortunate condition, and that she'd have to live with it.

But the pointed teeth were the least of poor Isabella's problems. Isabella also suffered from insomnia, and on some nights would leave home in the middle of the night to wander the woods. Around the same time that Isabella's insomnia kicked into overdrive, farmers began reporting attacks on their livestock. This went on for an unknown duration of time, but the story came to a head in a similar fashion to the movie *The Wolf Man*, which, if you'll recall, had Larry Talbot's father being the one to kill his son.

In this case, Isabella's sister, Sarah, watched Isabella slip into the night and followed her. Unbeknownst to them both, their mother also followed her daughters into the night, carrying a gun for protection. On this same night, a group of hunters was also out to get the animal attacking their livestock.

There are several variations as to what happened that night. Some are far-out enough to suggest that the hunters actually saw a werewolf and used silver bullets to shoot at it. Other, more down-to-earth variations of the story say that Isabella was simply spotted clutching a knife as she leered at some livestock in a sheep pasture in the distance. Mrs. Burt came on the scene just as Isabella was about to pounce and called at her to stop. Supposedly, Isabella turned to look at her and snarled like an animal. Then, one of the hunters shot Isabella. Or so that story goes. Another more interesting version goes that the men shot a wolf in the foot, and that Mrs. Burt later found Isabella, minus a hand, lying in a pool of her own blood.

In all versions, Isabella survives the gunshot wound and is sent off to Europe. Though said to be visiting relatives, in reality she was being treated by a doctor in Paris for lycanthropy, the condition of which causes a human being to believe that they are a wolf. And, considering that Isabella was said to have a keen interest in the occult and the supernatural, she might well have suffered from this affliction.

To cap off the story, while Isabella was away, the attacks on livestock ceased. When she returned, cured from her mental affliction, she lived out a normal life, passing away at the age of 70 in 1911. Upon her death, supposedly some of the area residents objected to her receiving a Christian burial, what with her having been a werewolf and all. However, cooler heads prevailed, and Isabella was buried in the local cemetery just like everyone else. Today, allegedly, her ghost can be seen roaming Ownes and Holmes Cemetery where she is buried.

Again, it's unknown how much of Isabella's story is true, and even modern-day relatives still debate what really happened. I think the real key in understanding this story is, when did it actually start to circulate? If it came about after the release of *The Wolf Man* in 1941, I would have to guess it was mostly fabricated based on the fact that it took place in Talbot County. Furthermore, the story is quite similar to *She-Wolf of London*, a little known Universal horror film from 1946. In that decidedly disappointing flick, the titular character is just a sleep-walker who thinks she's a wolf, much like the girl in this story. And, again, the climax of Isabella's own story reeks of *The Wolf Man*, where Larry Talbot's father finds his son in wolf form out in the woods. Ultimately we'll have to be content with wondering if art imitated life, or if it was the other way around.

Sources:

Roberts, Nancy. *Georgia Ghosts*. Blair, 1997.

Weatherly, David. *Peach State Monsters: Cryptids & Legends of Georgia*. Eerie Lights Publishing, 2021.

CHAPTER 26
LONG ISLAND LEAPER

I
n the late summer of 1909, Nassau County of Long Island, New York, experienced a flap of sightings of a very strange being. The man-thing sounded a bit like Spring Heeled Jack, though one witness compared him to Dracula. However, he never sucked anyone's blood (that we know of), nor did he seem to cause any significant physical harm to anyone. But something about the man's appearance definitely unsettled the populace, hence the stir he created in the news. The story was printed in numerous papers, but this particular one came from the August 16, 1906 edition of the *Tremont Times*:

FRIGHTENS LONG ISLAND LOVERS.
Strange Creature Roosts In Trees - Big Man Hunt Is Planned.

BALDWIN, L.I., July 29. - That a wild man lurks in the woods by this village there can be no possible doubt. Constable Stephen Petit led a posse into the haunts of this creature but was able to find only a few deserted nests in the trees where the unwelcome visitor had lodged. Residents of the section are in a state bordering on terror. They bar and bolt their doors at night and two or three of the inhabitants have set spring guns on their front porches.

Because the creature has been seen perched like a wild turkey the story has gained circulation that he has wings. Miss Sempronia Jenkins, principal of the Freeport high school, has called him Dracula, after the principal character in one of Bram Stoker's novels, and the watchword of all Nassau is "Dracula alive or dead."

Dracula has been wandering near the pumping station, which is used to supply a portion of Brooklyn. He has also appeared at dawn to Mr. Simpkin, who was gathering the products of his Plymouth Rocks. The wild man seized the rubber dating stamp with which Mr. Simpkin was about to imprint an egg, and with a fiendish cry tore across the railroad track and disappeared in a clump of blackberry bushes.

Haunts the Kissing Bridge.
Young persons who are accustomed to visit the kissing bridge at twilight now shun it, for the unpleasant experience of a Freeport couple there has alarmed the community. They were leaning against the rail when the wild man approached and laid a rough, heavy hand on the youth's shoulder, and then laughing in his face suddenly swung himself into the branches of a weeping willow which was on the overhanging bank of the stream.

Miss Conway, who lives at Oakview avenue, outside the main portion of this village declares that last Monday afternoon she saw a tall man emerge from the woods. His clothing, which was torn and threadbare, was black. His hair was intensely black, and he also wore a black mustache.

His eyes had a wild and restless expression, and she noted also that his feet, which were incased in patent leather shoes, seemed small and that he apparently had little or no toes. The wild man looked about him in every direction, and catching sight of an automobile, gave vent to ribald laughter and receded into the underbrush.

Wild men have been seen from time to time in this vicinity, for several sanatoriums for the weak-minded are with a radius of ten miles, but this is the first one who goes to roost. Rude platforms of branches on which he has been in the habit of sleeping are in evidence.

Unless Dracula is treed by the end of this week, preparations will be made for a man hunt next Sunday, and the woods will be filled with determined sportsmen.

As usual, there's not much one can do regarding these stories other than looking up the names involved to see if they at least were real. Constable Stephen Petit was indeed Sheriff of Nassau County for three years, among the many other hats the man wore. Overall, his activities are well-documented. As to the other named witnesses, I could find no verification that they existed, but considering that Petit was real, I imagine the rest of the witnesses were as well.

However, there's also something that I don't like about this story. In terms of the *Tremont Times* issue that I found this story in, it was printed on page six along with a number of other fairly incredulous stories. Perhaps it was a page devoted to odd, humorous stories in general, which doesn't have to mean that any of them were made up, but it's still discouraging. However, that said, I also found the story printed on a page of otherwise serious, credible news stories in the July 15, 1906 edition of *The Minneapolis Journal.*

SPRING HEELED JACK.

Real or not, the being sounds most like Spring Heeled Jack in its actions.[70] Like Jack, the Long Island Leaper was a humanoid capable of making superhuman leaps and bounds. The being wasn't dressed as oddly as Jack was, but it did dress in all black, which is ominous, and the mustache could be comparable to Jack's devilish goatee. Otherwise, this leaper is much more down to earth than Jack, who could also spew flames from his mouth and

[70] If you're reading this book out of order, Spring Heeled Jack was covered in the chapter entitled "Spring Heeled Jack Stateside".

sometimes had glowing eyes. However, like Jack, a story did begin to circulate that the Leaper had wings, which was likely just hearsay and nothing to seriously consider. As to the Long Island Leaper's other odd attributes, the fact that it literally nested in trees is also interesting. That he had abnormally small feet is also odd—if the small-footed man exiting the brush that Miss Conway reported was indeed the same man.

Unfortunately, there's not enough information or follow-up articles to determine if the Long Island Leaper was simply a wild man with the ability to make huge leaps or a supernatural being comparable to Spring Heeled Jack. However, the Long Island Leaper does have both predecessors and successors alike worth discussing. About two decades before the advent of the Long Island Leaper, a fire-breathing phantom haunted Long Island in the vicinity of Centerville in 1885. Actually, if you take the article at face value, it appears the being had also terrorized the area in 1880. See for yourself in the relevant portion of the article reprinted from Mysterious Universe:

...After a rest of five years, a specter with a tongue of fire has reappeared on the old Centerville race course, just south of Woodhaven, and men and women congregate every night to witness the strange sight. His ghostship appears promptly at a quarter to ten o'clock and departs at twelve minutes after eleven... There is a dispute whether the ghost wears a robe of white or a garment more the

THE CONEY ISLAND BAT MAN

It's possible that the 1880 sighting alluded to the in the article was related to this story, reported in September of 1880 in the *New York Times*:

> One day last week a marvelous apparition was seen near Coney Island. At the height of at least 1000 feet in the air a strange object was in the act of flying toward the New Jersey coast. It was apparently a man in bat's wings and improved frog's legs. The face of the man could be distinctly seen and he wore a cruel and determined expression.
>
> The movements made by the object closely resembled those of a frog in the act of swimming with his hind legs and flying with his front legs. When we add that this monster waved his wings in answer to the whistle of a locomotive and was of a deep black color, the alarming nature of the apparition can be imagined. The object was seen by many reputable persons and they all agree that it was a man engaged in flying toward New Jersey.

color of sheep's wool. But on one other point there is no disagreement – the ghost spits fire like a foundry chimney and leaves a sulphurous odor behind it... It moves along space like a feather in the wind, going a zigzag course. At regular intervals it spits fire. Scores of persons have followed in its wake without getting close enough for personal contact, and all declare that when the ghost comes to stop, it invariably says 'Whoa!'"[71]

LAWRENCE, LONG ISLAND CHURCH.

That same year in December, also in New York, this time in Lawrence, a similar being appeared:

The people of Lawrence, an aristocratic quarter of recent creation near Far Rockaway, were mystified and puzzled by the appearance of "a specter" in the belfry of the Methodist Episcopal Church. Men gathered in dark places every night to observe the strange sight. It flirts about the belfry in the most nimble fashion, one time ascending to the apex of the steeple and at another executing a dance on the slanting roof. It plays hide and seek in the lattice work of the bell room, enlarging and decreasing in size

---

[71] Paijmans, "Spring Heeled Jack in America," Mysterious Universe. http://mysteriousuniverse.org/2013/10/spring-heeled-jack-in-america/

according to the angle of observation. A remarkable thing is that it never appears on a Sunday night. Every night scores of persons walk or drive to the vicinity of the Lawrence Church to verify it. Some of these declare that the specter has followed them home and hung around their residences for hours. Last Saturday night the strange figure was more than usually active, and scores of persons kept their eyes fixed on it until, benumbed by the cold, they were driven home. Half the village declares that at precisely ten o'clock the bell was tolled. Immediately after the tolling, three hearty amens were heard, and then the specter flattened itself out on the roof. After a few minutes there was seen the liveliest skipping in and out of the lattice work, and then the phantom ran up and down the surface of the steeple, concluding by perching on the top, and disappearing in the direction of the graveyard.[72]

In 1889, the specter returned yet again in Wading River. The article reported that:

They have a lively ghost at Wading River...this Wading River specter keeps perfect silence and strikes terror to the beholders by darting fire at them out of its eyes... the figure's dress is smoky in color instead of pure white. At 11:55 o'clock P.M. the ghost appears in the churchyard and jumps around in the liveliest possible way,

---

[72] Ibid.

apparently trying to read the inscriptions on the tombstones and locate itself properly. At precisely 12 o'clock, M. the figure mounts to the top of a stone, lets go twelve fiery darts and disappears from view entirely. It rarely appears or disappears at the same point twice and the startled people do not know where to look for it, but they have no difficulty in locating it when the moments for the earth to open up and reveal the messenger from sheol arrives... They say that long before the fiery object took to practicing athletics in the graveyard it could be discerned playing hide and seek in the church belfry, and on one occasion the bell was rung violently at midnight..."[73]

It was recorded yet again three years later in 1892, this time dressed in white rather than black and spitting fire along Raymond Street in Brooklyn:

The good people living on Raymond Street in the vicinity of the jail are greatly excited over the reported visitation of an inhabitant of the other world that has been seen in and around the jail... A colored youth standing hard by was observed to remark, while his eyes danced with excitement: '...it wuz a great big thing, seven or eleven feet high, all dressed in white, with horns on its head.'...A business man in the immediate vicinity... said: '...Those who have seen it

---

[73] Ibid.

probably imagined it... I have heard it described as being anywhere from seven to twelve feet high, dressed in white; some say with fire shooting out of its mouth...[74]

In 1897 it was back again, carrying a lantern in true Spring Heeled Jack style in Auburn:

Auburn, N.Y., Aug. 5 – Hundreds of people have been greatly annoyed by the antics of a new kind of ghost. It is in the habit of appearing at 1 o'clock at night, and is tall, clothed in white and carries a lantern. It does not glide, as most specters do, but bounds like a kangaroo...rising from the center of the oat field a strange apparition, it was apparently the figure of a man clothed entirely in white. The ghostly figure stalked across the oat field, swinging a lantern in its hand. It advanced to the fence facing the round, and after flourishing his lantern up and down several times like a brakeman signaling a railroad train, the white figure gave a tremendous bound into the air and vanished from sight....About 10 o'clock the ghost appeared, carrying his lantern with him. The spectre made its appearance, apparently rising from the ground at the foot of a beech tree which stands at the west end of the field. The white robed figure dodged in and out, seen at one minute, the next lost to sight. After continuing his performance for a few minutes,

---

[74] Ibid.

the figure advanced boldly toward the astounded spectators. It came on with abounding movement, similar to that made by a kangaroo while in motion. When within a few feet of the spectators, the ghost stood motionless for a second, and after waving the lantern in the air three or four times, suddenly vanished from sight...

LONG ISLAND SCENE FROM THE EARLY 1900s.

This is the last sighting for a while of leaping beings in New York until the 1906 flap in Long Island. Though I was dubious of that sighting at first, the amount of previous encounters made me reconsider the 1906 Long Island Leaper story as being much more than just a jumping wild man. And the sightings didn't stop with the 1906 Leaper, either. Three years later, down south in Georgetown, Delaware, yet another leaper was sighted in 1909:

More than seven feet in height and swathed in a long black cloak, closely wrapped around its face, a new mystery has been exciting some parts of Georgetown, where it has followed women and young girls and jumped out from behind trees at them. The 'Devil in Black,' as it is called, first appeared several nights ago, when a dozen or so persons saw it during the course of the evening. From behind a tree it jumped at Mrs. William Curdy and sent her screaming with fright into a neighbor's house, while a daughter of Joseph Carnel also was chased by the mysterious stranger until she fell almost fainting into Fred Rust's grocery store. The men of the neighborhood, informed of the affair, led by William Curdy, ran across fields, jumped fences and through back yards, with the 'Devil' but a few yards ahead of them, but, while crossing the big ditch known as the Savannah, the figure completely disappeared and, despite search, could not be found. Again it was seen by several young girls and last night it made its appearance and was seen closely by Mrs. Carn Josephs, who heard a noise as she passed her woodshed. She turned to look and distinctly saw the 'Devil' walk out of the shed and after her. Almost fainting with fear she ran screaming into the house, while her husband ran into the yard with his gun and fired at the tall figure, which was plainly distinguished at the woodshed. In a second it was gone with no trace of injury from the gun. Many superstitious declare that bullets cannot hit it, but some of the more determined men declare it is the work of a practical joker and expect to put a load of shot into it at their first opportunity."

The end of that article poses what I would call the "bottom-line" question, that being, were these tricksters multiple human pranksters or a single, bonafide supernatural being? Let's go over the facts once more. Over the course of about thirty years, New Yorkers witnessed humanoid beings capable of great leaps and bounds. In some cases, these beings were even said to be able to breathe fire, something that no normal human being could do. So while it is within the realm of possibility that a prankster could have made some impressive leaps and bounds, and that also perhaps witnesses exaggerated stories to give the perpetrator supernatural traits, what is odder yet is the thirty year span. Are we to believe that for thirty years one man went about imitating Spring-Heeled Jack? After all, wouldn't he eventually get too old to engage in the acrobatic acts required? Or are we to believe that several different men over the decades chose to perpetrate the same prank over and over again? Or, is it simpler to surmise that perhaps the being was simply a Spring Heeled Jack-like entity? Of the two explanations, the supernatural one is actually the more plausible.

Sources:

Paijmans, Theo. "Spring Heeled Jack in America," Mysterious Universe. http://mysteriousuniverse.org/2013/10/spring-heeled-jack-in-america/

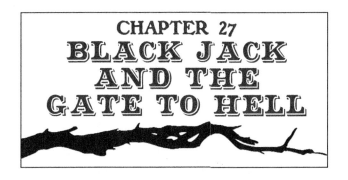

CHAPTER 27
BLACK JACK
AND THE
GATE TO HELL

Since earlier was covered Jesse James and the Phantom Rider and the tale of Billy the Kid's restless bones, it would be remiss to not include the tale of Black Jack Ketchum's ghost and its association with the Philmont Scout Ranch. Not as well-known as either James or the Kid, Black Jack's biggest claim to fame comes via his botched execution in 1901.

Born on Halloween day in 1863 as Thomas Edward Ketchum, he eventually earned the nickname of Black Jack when he began a life of crime in the 1890s. Black Jack rubbed elbows with other famous outlaws of the day, like those belonging to the Hole in the Wall Gang famous for Butch Cassidy, the Sundance Kid, and Kid Curry, among others.

CLAYTON, NEW MEXICO C.1904.

In 1899, Black Jack was wounded and eventually captured after a botched train robbery. He was sentenced to hang in Clayton, New Mexico, a town where nobody had ever been hung before. "Please dig my grave very deep. All right; hurry up," Black Jack reportedly said from the gallows. When the executioner activated the trap door, Black Jack dropped and the noose ripped his head from his body. This happened for two reasons. For starters, Black Jack had "let himself go," as we would say in modern terms, and had gained weight while in prison. But, more importantly, due to Clayton's inexperience in hangings, the rope they used was too long.

As such, Black Jack's execution became one of the more famous hangings of the Old West. Photographs were taken of the headless body, and the head was later sewn back on for viewings and he was eventually buried in the Clayton Cemetery. But, of course, with a notorious hanging like that, that wasn't the last anyone saw of Black Jack Ketchum.

Many years later, in the vicinity of the Philmont Scout Ranch in northeastern New Mexico, a boy scout troop was backpacking across the mountains to visit sites of historical interest, like an abandoned gold mine and a ghost town. They also visited a large rock overhang hideout alleged to have been used by Black Jack Ketchum. The boys wanted to camp right under the overhang, but the scoutmaster wouldn't let them and insisted they camp at the designated spot nearby.

BLACK JACK ON THE GALLOWS C.1901.

That night, five of the boys snuck away to the hideout to set up their own camp. Under the overhang they built a fire and discussed their journey so far. Eventually, they all fell asleep. One of the boys, the unnamed storyteller of this tale, claims that noises from the bushes nearby woke him up. Upon waking, he experienced the phenomena known as sleep paralyses, where he was conscious but unable to move or speak.

THOMAS KETCHUM IN LIFE.

Then he saw the source of the noise: a filthy, dirty cowboy dressed in all black. His face glistened red, as though scorched by the sun even in the darkness of night. The figure was mostly solid, though a few parts of his body appeared to be translucent. The boy took note of the man's clothes, which looked tattered and ancient as though they were from the days of the Wild West, and also of the fact that the man carried a revolver. Luckily for the boy, the phantom cowboy didn't seem to notice him. In fact, it was as if the boy was seeing into another dimension occupied by the cowboy.

The boy claimed that a mist began to emanate from a tree line across from a small stream. From within the mist he could hear the shouts of men and also gunfire. The cowboy turned his attention to the noise and fired his revolver into the direction of the mist. The cowboy then ran right to where the boy slept and began firing while standing right above him. During the shooting, the cowboy was hit by a bullet in the shoulder. As he returned fire, the terrified scout watched as the bullet casings fell to the ground next to where he lay.

Suddenly, for the first time, the gunslinger noticed the scout beneath his feet. The outlaw looked nearly as startled as the boy and muttered, "You're not supposed to be here." After that the cowboy ghost disappeared into thin air. The next morning the boy told his fellow scouts what had happened, though they simply brushed it off as him pulling a prank. Later in the trip, upon stopping in an Old West-themed saloon, the boy saw a picture on the wall of the cowboy from his experience. It was Black Jack Ketchum.

And while this may sound like a typical campfire story, there are two aspects that elevate it to something more significant. First is the setting, Philmont Ranch, in the vicinity of Urraca Mesa. Though relatively obscure outside of New Mexico, Urraca Mesa might well have been the real-life inspiration behind the gate to hell featured in *Ghostbusters: Afterlife* (2021).

**SPIRAL PETROGLYPH AT PHILMONT
SCOUT RANCH–IS IT A PORTAL?**

Urraca Mesa—named for urracas, or magpies— stretches two miles long by a half a mile wide and in some maps even bears a vague resemblance to a human skull. It is dotted with ponderosa pines and various Native American ruins. The most unique of these are two wooden cat totems, of which there used to be four. This is because, according to Native American lore, Urraca Mesa is a gateway to the underworld. Many years ago, in the days of the long since vanished Anasazi, a battle was fought between the peoples of the surface world and the evil spirits of the underworld. The forces of humanity prevailed against the evil spirits and somehow forced them through a portal located in the mesa and then sealed it back up.

After this, a powerful medicine man created the aforementioned cat totems to seal the doorway. Originally, there were four, and now there are only two. This might be why Urraca Mesa is plagued by so many ghostly occurrences. Supposedly, when the last two totems fall, the gates to hell will open once again. But until the floodgates open, spook hunters can still take a peek at spectral stampedes of cattle along with phantom Native American riders and a few cowboys.

TOOTH OF TIME FORMATION AT PHILMONT SCOUT RANCH.

VAMPIRES, MUMMIES, AND WEREWOLVES
OF THE WILD WEST

Rather than ghosts, some think these spectral figures are really glimpses into the past. Case in point, in 2003 an account appeared online telling of a former Philmont staff member who camped atop the mesa one night. They awoke during a rainstorm and witnessed "a blue vertical line appear a few feet above the ground and then drop like a curtain." Out of this apparent time portal came through a group of Native Americans charging on horseback. The man then ran away in terror and accidentally ran into a barbed-wire fence and bled to death... which is, unfortunately, exactly why this is befitting of an online tale. Because, if the man died, how did anyone learn his story? Perhaps his ghost told it.

While the above story is a bit discouraging, it seems to be based on more credible accounts which also whisper of strange blue lights along the mesa. Others tell of missing time similar to UFO abductions and battery-operated equipment draining at alarming rates. Some attribute this to the mesa's unusually high amounts of magnetite and iron, though others claim a supernatural property.

If the story of the scout who saw Black Jack is to be believed, then it would seem that the area is home to some sort of time portal. I say this because, as the scout was putting up his bedroll the morning after the encounter, he found six shell casings in the dirt next to him. Were these perhaps shell casings from the Old West, you muse? Yes and no, apparently. The boy naturally swiped the shells to keep as a memento. When he had them examined by a gun expert, the gunsmith confirmed that they were indeed from 1878, but appeared to be brand new at the same time. Furthermore, the gunpowder used to fire the bullets was also of an old variety, but the casings appeared to have been fired very recently as gunpowder could still be smelt on them...

Sources:

Smith, Mike. "Hell on a Mesa." My Strange New Mexico.

Weiser-Alexander, Kathy. "Black Jack Ketchum Lives On! – A Ghost Story." Legends of America. (updated November 2021)

https://www.legendsofamerica.com/blackjack-ghost/

CHAPTER 28
BURIAL GROUND BEAST

or all the skeptics and doubters of these stories, sometimes you have to admit that the coincidences within them are too much. And it's always the little things. A good example is the Crosswicks Monster of 1882, which was a theropod-type dinosaur found hiding in a hollowed-out tree, just like a similar dinosaur monster from all the way down in Oklahoma. Hoaxers and yarn spinners back then usually weren't knowledgeable or clever enough to cross-reference their stories in such a way, especially in the pre-internet age.

In this story's case, we have similar monsters being sighted in similar locations only one state away from one another. Since Illinois borders

Wisconsin to the south, I found it fascinating that Illinois had what sounded to be a werewolf sighting similar to Wisconsin's Beast of Bray Road all the way back in 1879.

**BEAST OF BRAY ROAD ILLUSTRATION
BY LINDA GODFREY C.1991.**

Though the story of the Bray Road Beast's journey into the public consciousness begins in the late 1980s thanks to journalist Linda Godfrey, eventually Godfrey discovered that the werewolf dated back to the 1930s. Late one night in 1936, night watchman Mark Shackleman was on his way to work at the St. Coletta School for Exceptional Children. Walking across a field where an old Native American Burial ground was located, he spied a strange dog-like animal digging into the mounds. He could also smell rotten meat. Suddenly, the wolf-like being turned to look at him and stood up on its hind legs, making it about six feet tall. Thankfully for Shackleman, the beast ran away into the wild.

To the south of Wisconsin, in the neighboring state of Illinois, a similar werewolf-like beast was sighted on a Native American burial ground in the summer of 1879 near Rock River, Illinois. The story was published in the *New Orleans Times-Picayune* on August 3, 1879:

A Mysterious Monster.

Remarkable Midnight Gunning by Two Geneseo Hunters for a Strange Beast – Escape of the Varmint.

[Correspondence Chicago Times.]

GENESEO, Ill., July 30. — Esil Clouse, a well known merchant of this city, and a man named Hefner, from Rock Island, Ill., met with an adventure in the Rock River forest, adjacent to Penney's Slough, seven miles north of here, on last Friday night [July 25], that savors strongly of the marvelous. Everybody in this city knows

Clouse. He is a sober, quiet, honest young married man.

Clouse and Hefner were fishing in Penney's Slough on Friday night, and about midnight they were startled by a series of the most hideous yells, emanating from the old Indian burying-ground, just over the edge of the precipitous bluff that rises a few rods back from the slough. Hefner said: "There is that animal again." On being asked to explain, he related that he had seen a large, strange animal in that neighborhood about a year previous. Both then seized their guns (double-barreled breech-loaders) and, leaving a young man named Lawson in charge of the camp, clambered up the bluff, and were soon in the old burying-ground.

Each had a lantern, and by the light of these soon saw an animal about the size of a large Newfoundland dog standing erect on its hind feet on one of the Indian graves. Clouse says that the beast had no hair, but seemed to be covered with large bony plates or scales. Two large white stripes ran down his back. His head was small, and surmounted by a pair of long pointed ears, which he flapped up and down with great facility. He stood and stared fiercely at the men, blinking in the lights of the lanterns. He pounded his breast vehemently and with his fore paws. Both Clouse and Hefner fired into his body with BB shot from a distance of about three rods. The effect was to knock the animal over; but he was immediately on his feet again, and howling like a demon. Clouse describes the sound of the shot as they struck the body to be similar to striking a hollow stump. They gave him another load each. He then took to racing frantically up and down an old hollow tree, about the center of the grave yard. While this was going on they gave him in all a dozen charges of heavy shot. Finally he ran into a hole in the tree. Determined to kill him if possible, the men ran to the camp and procured a couple of axes, with which they soon felled the hollow and rotten tree. The screams of the brute as the tree fell were absolutely horrible. He rushed from his lair and into the forest, returning several times and making at the men as if to attack them. He finally departed and was seen no more. The men visited the ground next day, but could detect no trace of blood. In the hollow of the tree they found the sleeve of a coat, a pocket and some buttons. Bear-traps and various devices are now planted about the brute's haunts, and hopes are entertained that he may be captured.

Though it's odd that the beast had what appeared to be scales rather than hair, the comparison was still made immediately to a Newfoundland dog, as opposed to any other similar sized animal, which I find interesting. Then there's the pointed ears which sound to be canine-like. I also took note of how they described the creature as "standing erect on its hind feet" which indicates the beast wasn't taken to be bipedal or humanoid in stance. The usage of the term hind legs also brings to mind a dog rather than a primate or human. There is also the mention of "forepaws" rather than hands.

ROCK RIVER AREA, ILLINOIS.

The hollow tree is also interesting for a few reasons. If one wants to go full werewolf in regard to this story, they could surmise that the "sleeve of a coat, a pocket and some buttons" belonged to the monster in its human form. Or, it could have belonged to someone that the monster killed and drug back to its lair. I also find it interesting how many monsters use hollowed-out trees as lairs. In many myths, hollowed-out trees are also home to fairies, gnomes, and other supernatural entities.

Surprisingly, when one searches out the mythical animals and monsters of the Rock River region, the Winnebago Native American tribe has an oral tradition stating that when their people and the Potawatomi camped along the river banks, they encountered a terrible water demon. They said that it had horns on its head, a long tail, great jaws and fangs, and a snake-like body.[75] I halfway wonder if the monster's horns could correlate to the pointed ears seen by the two men in 1897, and if perhaps the scaly body lines up with the description of the Native American monster having the body of a snake? Of course, it's by no means a dead-ringer, but it's interesting nonetheless. And, the creature was sighted at a Native American burial ground, and it would be interesting to know if that burial ground belonged to either the Winnebago or Potawatomi tribe.

POSTCARD ALLEGEDLY DEPICTING WINNEBGAO TRIBE OF WISCONSIN.

The Winnebago monster sounded quite a bit larger than the creature seen in 1879, as it was large enough to swallow a deer or a man whole. (Perhaps

---

[75] I suppose this monster could be some type of variation of the Piasa Bird of Illinois, but the Piasa Bird had wings, and accounts of the Rock River demon didn't.

273

the 1879 beast was a juvenile? Actually, if I were to peg this story on anything, it would be John Keel's ultraterrestrial theory, that claimed that these cosmic beings purposely take the form of area myths. And, the Winnebago peoples did make offerings to this monster, which I also find interesting. For the sake of argument, let's say the monster was indeed a sinister ultraterrestrial. If that were the case, then why wouldn't it take the form of a local legend?

Or, perhaps there is no relation at all to the cryptid sighted in 1879 and the demon said to inhabit the depths of Rock River. Even though the 1879 cryptid certainly wasn't a traditional werewolf, maybe it was some kind of offshoot related to the one seen haunting the burial mounds of Bray Road years later? In any case, it's interesting that we have two accounts, relatively close to one another involving a werewolf-like animal associated with a Native American burial ground.

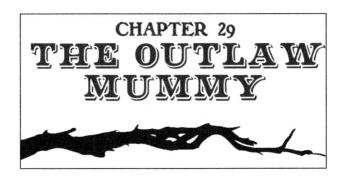

CHAPTER 29
THE OUTLAW MUMMY

In life, Elmer McCurdy didn't amount to much, but in death was another story. In life, McCurdy was a second-class outlaw, perhaps born too late as he was too young to participate in the heyday of the Wild West. McCurdy was born in 1880 and began his inept reign of terror at the age of 31. I say inept because McCurdy's endeavors at bank and train robbery weren't terribly successful. Humorously, McCurdy had mishaps when he turned to using explosives during his crimes, often overestimating how much nitroglycerin was needed.[76]

For instance, in March of 1911, McCurdy and three outlaw companions successfully stopped a

---

[76] He had been trained to use nitroglycerin for demolition purposes during his time in the army.

train along the Iron Mountain-Missouri Pacific carrying $4,000. However, McCurdy rigged the safe with too much nitroglycerin and the safe, along with the money, was completely destroyed. Instead, McCurdy and his pals had to make due with the remains of silver coins which had melded into the safe's frame in the explosion. A similar incident occurred when McCurdy robbed a Kansas bank and destroyed the bank's interior.

McCurdy's last hurrah occurred that October in Okesa, Oklahoma. McCurdy and his compatriots set their sights on a train carrying $400,000, only they stopped the passenger car rather than the one containing the money. So instead they stole a measly $46 total from the mail clerk, some whiskey, and the conductor's watch. A newspaper later joked that it was "one of the smallest in the history of train robbery."

McCurdy sulked off to a friend's ranch to drink away his sorrows, and that's where he was captured. Early in the morning of October 7th, when McCurdy was still sleeping one off, three sheriffs tracked him down using bloodhounds and found him in a barn. In an interview in the October 8, 1911 edition of the *Daily Examiner*, Sheriff Bob Fenton said:

> It began just about 7 o'clock. We were standing around waiting for him to come out when the first shot was fired at me. It missed me and he then turned his attention to my brother, Stringer Fenton. He shot three times at Stringer and when my brother got under cover he turned his

attention to Dick Wallace. He kept shooting at all of us for about an hour. We fired back every time we could. We do not know who killed him ... (on the trail) we found one of the jugs of whiskey which was taken from the train. It was about empty. He was pretty drunk when he rode up to the ranch last night.

McCurdy's unremarkable career had come to an end. Similar to the case of David E. George (alias John Wilkes Booth), who died in Oklahoma a decade ago, McClurdy's body went unclaimed at the undertakers. Perhaps recalling the success of the Booth mummy, Joseph L. Johnson, the owner and undertaker, embalmed the body with an arsenic-based preservative. He then gave poor McCurdy a shave, dressed him in a suit, and stored him in the back of the funeral home. Then, taking another page from the Booth Mummy, Johnson decided to exploit him. However, Johnson was sly enough to realize that the McCurdy Mummy wasn't as big a deal as the Booth Mummy, who, after all, may have killed Abraham Lincoln. As such, Johnson humorously dressed his mummy in· street clothes, placed a rifle in his hands, and called him "The Bandit Who Wouldn't Give Up" in reference to McCurdy's numerous failed robberies.[77] Johnson would then charge folks a whole nickel to come gawk at it.

---

[77] His other names included "The Mystery Man of Many Aliases", "The Oklahoma Outlaw", and "The Embalmed Bandit".

PHOTOGRAPHED BY W. J. BOAG PAWHUSKA OKLA.

The mummy became so popular that it attracted offers from carnivals who wished to purchase it, but Johnson refused. Upon Johnson's refusal, the carnival owners got creative. In October of 1916, two men claiming to be McCurdy's brothers showed up and requested the body of their "brother" so they could give him a proper burial. Feeling it was the decent thing to do, Johnson allowed them to take the body back home. Only they didn't. One of the men was none other than James Patterson himself, of Great Patterson Carnival Shows (the other man was his brother Charles). The Patterson brothers then began exploiting Johnson's old mummy as "The Outlaw Who Would Never Be Captured Alive" in a traveling circus. This lasted until 1922 when Patterson sold his circus to Louis Sonney.

Appropriately, Sonney featured the McCurdy Mummy in his traveling Museum of Crime, which also included wax replicas of Bill Doolin and Jesse James. By 1928, McCurdy changed hands again to be a part of the official sideshow of the Trans-American Footrace. Then, in 1933, McCurdy was exploited by a man named Dwain Esper to promote his exploitation film *Narcotic.* Poor McCurdy was himself now playing a part as the body of a "dead dope fiend" on display in the theater lobby. Esper claimed that the dead man had been gunned down after robbing a drug store to support his habit. As it turned out, this was McCurdy's start in the acting business. It was also at this point that he was less of an embalmed corpse and more of a mummy, as his skin had hardened a great deal and the body began to shrivel. (Esper claimed that the skin's appearance was due to his drug use!)

LOUIS SONNEY AND HIS TRAVELING SHOW.

The mummy was put in storage in a Los Angeles warehouse and resurfaced again in 1964, when it was lent to filmmaker David F. Friedman for his movie, *She Freak,* released in 1967. The next year, the body was part of a $10,000 sale along with some wax figures to the Hollywood Wax Museum. McCurdy then got a gig at a show at Mount Rushmore; only he was damaged during a windstorm that blew off the tips of his ears, fingers, and toes. Poor McCurdy was then dropped for looking "too gruesome" and not looking lifelike enough to exhibit. No longer in the bigtime, poor McCurdy was sold off to The Pike, an amusement park in Long Beach, California. He worked there until 1976, but like some of the more fortunate actors, McCurdy was destined for a comeback.

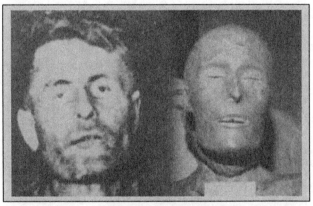

MCCURDY SHORTLY AFTER DEATH AND AS A MUMMY.

McCurdy's big break came from sheer luck, as it turned out. In December of 1976, the crew of *The Six Million Dollar Man* TV series was filming scenes for their "Carnival of Spies" episode at The Pike. McCurdy was just hanging around set, literally from a makeshift gallows, when one of the crew thought he was just a nobody and decided to move him out of the way. To his shock, the arm of what he assumed to be a plastic dummy broke right off, exposing bone and dried out muscle tissue. Seeing as how they had a real body on their hands, the crew called the police. An autopsy was performed, and of all things, a ticket stub found in the mouth helped the authorities uncover the mummy's identity. The stub was for Louis Sonney's Museum of Crime, and so the police contacted Sonney's son, Dan, who was able to confirm that the body was that of McCurdy.

Though McCurdy didn't get to appear on *The Six Million Dollar Man*, he got something much better: a proper burial. McCurdy made headlines more significantly than he ever had before, and funeral homes were now offering to bury him for free. Ultimately, he was shipped back to Oklahoma under the care of the Indian Territory Posse of Oklahoma Westerns. On April 22, 1977, a funeral procession took McCurdy to the Boot Hill section of the Summit View Cemetery in Guthrie, Oklahoma. Three hundred people attended his graveside service, and appropriately, he was buried next to his old pal Bill Doolin. The two didn't know each other in life, but McCurdy had toured with Doolin's wax mannequin on the road. Knowing how people could be with old outlaws, two feet of concrete were poured over his casket, an honor usually afforded to sensational outlaws like Billy the Kid. So, as it turned out, in his own strange way, McCurdy had finally made the "big time."

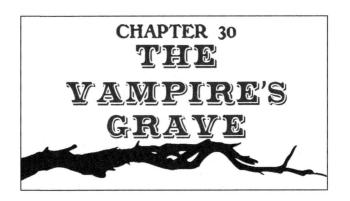

CHAPTER 30
THE VAMPIRE'S GRAVE

Much like the Lafayette "vampire" of Colorado is the "vampire" of a small graveyard in Dalby Springs, Bowie County, Texas. Cedar Grove Cemetery, aptly named, is tucked away in a tree grove and is well hidden.[78] It's far off the beaten path and can only be reached via a bumpy old wagon trail. The small cemetery boasts only about 20 graves and was first used in the mid-1800s, and the last burial took place in 1903.

---

[78] The first church there was built in 1839, so presumably that's when the graveyard sprouted as well. Also, the cemetery was originally known as Pleasant Grove Cemetery.

At the back of the cemetery is the "Vampire's Grave," so-called because it lacks a name and is very, very spooky. The plot is six by eight feet in dimensions, and the gate is six feet high. The grave is fenced in and has an iron stake driven right in the middle of it. Or at least it used to. The iron gate has been removed due to adventurous teenagers entering the cage—presumably due to the vampire legend—and getting trapped within it. The stake, too, has since been taken away, possibly out of fear of someone injuring themselves on it. [79] Or maybe a souvenir hunter dislodged it in hopes of resurrecting the alleged vampire. In any case, local lore held that the stake was a bit like Excalibur, as all teens who did their best to remove it failed.

There's another strange detail about the burial plot. Allegedly, for a time, there were two torches located at the grave. In her article on the Dalby Vampire for *The East Texas Journal*, Greta Reeves quoted a source who claimed that "there were two flame holders atop two poles of the fence, at the back of the 'cage.'" And that "the flames burned throughout several nights of the year until they were stolen, taken away." [80] Who lit these flames and kept them going all night is still a mystery.

Another strange detail was dropped by the same source, stating that the grave ran on a north to south line, the opposite of a traditional Christian burial. This was done, she said, so that the vampire

---

[79] It was last seen sometime around the year 2000.
[80] Reeves, "Vampire Legend Haunts Dalby Springs Back Road," *East Texas Journal.*

VAMPIRES, MUMMIES, AND WEREWOLVES
OF THE WILD WEST

wouldn't see the Lord approaching on Judgement
Day per traditions of the era.

CEDAR GROVE CEMETERY, WITH
VAMPIRE'S GRAVE IN BACKGROUND.

To better understand the vampire, we should
first delve into the history of the area where it is
buried. Dalby Springs began in the 1830s upon the
arrival of the Warren Dalby family, who discovered
springs on their property known for their mineral
content. The mineral-rich water quickly became
known for its medicinal properties, thus leading to
the construction of housing for those seeking its
health benefits in the 1850s. By 1860, a post office
followed, and in the mid-1880s, the population
reached its peak with 250 people. By the early

1900s, people began to learn of better cures for their ailments and quit coming to the area. At some point, the original church burnt down in the early 1900s and was later rebuilt. Today, the church still stands and about 100 residents or so remain in the area.

DALBY SPRINGS METHODIST CHURCH. BUILT OF KNOTLESS PINE LUMBER IN 1888. FIRST HOUSE OF WORSHIP BUILT BY CONGREGATION WHO HAD BEEN WORSHIPPING SINCE 1839 IN HOMES, GROVES AND SCHOOL. DURING THIS TIME THE TOWN OF DALBY SPRINGS EMERGED FROM FARMLAND AND GREW INTO A SUMMER HEALTH SPA. RECORDED TEXAS HISTORIC LANDMARK — 1966

DALBY SPRINGS HISTORICAL MARKER.

But why the legend of the vampire? Did the unmarked grave perhaps belong to someone suffering from tuberculosis à la Mercy Brown? Or could the vampire legend stem from the waters themselves? A quote from a Jesse Suttles on TexasLegends.com mentions that at one point the waters of Dalby Springs were actually red! This was in the 1950s and Suttles said, "The water from the well was dark red. It didn't smell very good. If you put the water in a glass jug, over time the inside of the jug would turn a dark rusty color. I guess it was from sulfur in the water or another mineral."[81]

81 http://www.texasescapes.com/EastTexasTowns/Dalby-Springs-Texas.htm

VAMPIRES, MUMMIES, AND WEREWOLVES OF THE WILD WEST

Greta Reeves may have found a more logical explanation in her research. Though she can't be certain that this was the name on the unmarked vampire's grave, she did find an entry of an Eliziz Williams born in 1797 and buried at Cedar Grove on October 31, 1879. Perhaps children simply saw the death date and decided the woman must have been a vampire? (Conversely, Texas Gravestone.org identifies the birthdate for Eliziz Williams as October 31, 1797, and she died on March 10, 1879.) And, Reeves did manage to find a grave for a Mrs. Williams (first name illegible) right next to the spot where the iron fence used to be. Another source told Reeves that all the burial records burned with the first church and that she believed the vampire legend was created by a caretaker to scare away possible vandals. (The logic in this is somewhat flawed, as stories of a vampire are instead what would likely draw vandals and thrill-seekers!)[82]

Just as I was about to label the case of the Texas Vampire a tall tale with no real supernatural activity to back it up, I came across the work of paranormal researcher Melba Goodwyn, who visited the cemetery on several occasions, and on two of them, very strange things happened. In her book, *Ghost*

---

[82] The cemetery is quite hard to find and is apparently mistaken for the Red Hill Cemetery south of the town of New Boston, twelve miles away from Cedar Grove Cemetery. Ironically, Red Hill Cemetery has its own "vampire" or ghost that is said to repose in a mausoleum. But it's thought this tale was inspired by Cedar Grove's vampire.

Worlds, Goodwyn recounted seeing a white fog enshroud the grave and experiencing paralyses at the grave before she snapped out of it and fled the cemetery. She was with her daughter, who claimed she could hear beautiful harp music coming from near the grave. She grabbed her mother's hand in a strong, steely grasp and tried to drag her into the white fog. Goodwyn managed to snap her daughter out of it and take her back to the car so they could leave. Later in the car, her daughter had the "missing time" experience common to alien abductions and fairy encounters in that she could not remember the incident at all.

Sometime later, Goodwyn brought a whole team of fellow paranormal investigators with her to study the grave. Her book *Chasing Graveyard Ghosts* provides one of the best write-ups on the vampire ever. According to Goodwyn, one will feel an unsettling chill the moment they walk into the cemetery, which she notes is on the 33rd parallel. Just as aliens and ghosts have a penchant for showing up at 3:30 A.M., strange things tend to occur on the 33rd parallel more so than others. Roswell, New Mexico, is located along this line as is Mt. Hermon in the Holy Land, where angels descended from the skies during the days of Enoch. Due to being situated on the 33rd parallel, it is even rumored that the upper-echelon, more occult driven Masons use the vampire's grave for arcane rituals.

Contrary to theories that the vampire story was made up by local teenagers—or elderly caretakers hoping to scare teenagers away—Goodwyn stated that she found quite a few elderly residents who do indeed believe the vampire story and are reluctant to talk about it, as if it's taboo. It was Goodwyn who brought the EVP and recorded the startling voice mentioned earlier. She also reported that a glowing red orb with menacing "eyes" was sighted. They could also hear the flapping of unseen wings somewhere as well. Eventually the terror mounted until Goodwyn and her team literally ran from the cemetery.

Goodwyn also claimed that the grave isn't the burial site of one vampire, but a whole family. Goodwyn postulated an imaginative theory as to what would bring the vampires to the area. While I had earlier mused that perhaps someone with a blood disease had begotten the vampire rumors, Goodwyn wondered if vampires moved to the health resort to take advantage of all the ill people there. After all, they would be too weak to ward them off, and when they died, it wouldn't be unexpected since they were ill. Goodwyn further went on to wonder if the removal of the stake removed the vampire or vampires plural? She wondered if the removal of the stake was why the place felt so haunted when she and her team investigated the area.

Though she doesn't give an exact source (presumably a local told her), she says that in the late 1800s a family of foreigners moved into the area. None of them except for the father could speak English, and his was very limited. For whatever reason, the family was suspected of being vampires and they were murdered and then buried in the cemetery, or so the story goes.

In recent years, a YouTube user, SafariClubUSA, uploaded a video of the cemetery. In the comments below, one user, Teresa Lynn, mentioned how the corners of the grave had upside-down crosses on them![83] The cage as it appears in the video is definitely creepy too. In 2010, SafariClubUSA made a nighttime visit to Cedar Grove Cemetery and filmed some mysterious bones near the grave. When they returned in the daylight to get a better idea of what the bones were, they were gone. Like the Lafayette Vampire, a recording was taken one night by a paranormal investigator, and the voice allegedly could be heard saying, "Come to the end of the row where the dead plague the living."

Though the simplest explanation is that people simply made up the vampire tale, you also have to ask yourself, why in the world would someone drive a metal stake right in the middle of an unmarked grave? You have to admit, it does make you wonder...

---

[83] SafariClubUSA, Vampire in Texas?, August 23, 2009.
https://www.youtube.com/watch?v=rk1zvBmdh1Y

Sources:

Goodwyn, Melba. *Chasing Graveyard Ghosts: Investigations of Haunted & Hallowed Ground.* Llewellyn Publications, 2011

---------------------------- *Ghost Worlds: A Guide to Poltergeists, Portals, Ecto-Mist, & Spirit Behavior.* Llewellyn Publications, 2007.

Reeves, Greta. "Vampire Legend Haunts Dalby Springs Back Road." *East Texas Journal* (July 12, 2018)

SafariClubUSA. "Vampire in Texas?" August 23, 2009. https://www.youtube.com/watch?v=rkIzvBmdh1Y

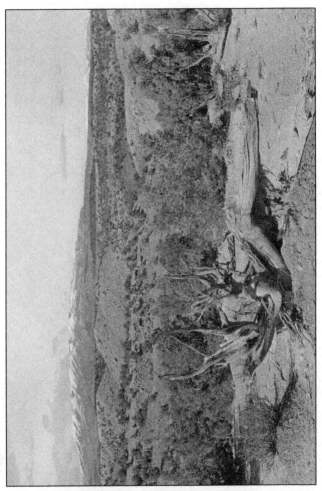

DUSCHESNE COUNTY, UTAH
BY JOHN VACHON APRIL 1942.
(LIBRARY OF CONGRESS)

POSTSCRIPT
THE ORIGINS OF SKINWALKER RANCH

It's become a bit of tradition to end each of these books with a special chapter or postscript detailing a fantastic location. The first book uncovered a hidden valley in the Grand Canyon full of pygmy horses and dinosaur petroglyphs, while the second featured a tropical oasis populated by mammoths and dinosaurs in the frozen Yukon. The third detailed a saurian-infested swamp in the Florida Everglades, and the fourth book explored several real lost worlds in South America plus Acambaro, Mexico.

I thought with this book I might have to finally break tradition. After all, those were all dinosaur inhabited "lost worlds" and it seemed there was no equivalent for the types of monsters covered in this book. And yet, somehow, I had forgotten about Skinwalker Ranch. Of all the haunted spots in America, none of them can compare to the Skinwalker Ranch of Utah. Though the name suggests a connection solely to werewolves, in actuality, it runs the full gamut of UFO, cryptid, and werewolf sightings!

Stories of the strange ranch rose to prominence in the mid-1990s when the new owners began seeing disturbing things on the property. UFOs, glowing orbs of light, and portals could be seen in the skies regularly. Cattle were often found mutilated with surgical precision, much in the style of the late 1970s cattle mutilation flap. But, most important to the ranch's namesake, they also saw gigantic wolves said to be four times larger than a normal wolf in addition to traditional skinwalker-like creatures.

To the uninitiated, this might seem like too much. After all, UFOs don't mix it up with werewolves, do they? Not traditionally they don't, and not in most European folklore. But there are certain places on Earth that experts have dubbed "window areas". Much like Urraca Mesa, covered a few chapters ago, certain areas are hotspots not only for UFOs and ghosts, but also for mystery creatures. UFOs have even been seen over Loch Ness in Scotland, for instance, though most people don't know this. Researchers like Jacques Vallée (*Passport to Magonia: From Folklore to Flying Saucers*) and John Keel (*The Mothman*

Prophecies) were among the first to connect the dots that most all things that "go bump in the night" seem to be related in some way. Keel took note of the fact that in addition to the cryptid-like Mothman, UFOs, ghosts, and Men in Black were sighted all over Point Pleasant, West Virginia, during the Mothman flap of the late 1960s. Similarly, Vallée was one of the first to point out the parallels between ancient fairy lore and modern UFO abduction cases.

So, the more one becomes accustomed to the unexplained, the more one realizes that all of these strange beings and creatures seem to be connected somehow, which oddly enough extends to skinwalkers and UFOs, or "sky beings" as Native Americans might call their occupants.

In 1994, what is now known as the Skinwalker Ranch, but was then known as the old Myers Ranch, was purchased by Terry and Gwen Sherman to run cattle on. As stated earlier, many of the cattle ended up dead, either from UFO-like mutilations or from attacks by mysterious, wolf-like predators. In fact, the Shermans got shed of the place by 1996 it proved so stressful on them and sold it to Robert Bigelow, owner of the National Institute for Discovery Science (NIDS). For ten years, NIDS accumulated what Charles Fort would have called the "damned data" as they made a study of literal monsters. Since then, Skinwalker Ranch has nearly gained as much notoriety as places like Roswell, New Mexico, and the aforementioned home of Mothman, Point Pleasant, West Virginia.

But what is it that makes Skinwalker Ranch such a haunted locale? Going all the way back to the Trail of Tears, some say that the Navajo cursed a certain portion of the land in the Uinta Basin which today serves as the Ute reservation. The Ute even call this area the Path of the Skinwalker and mount animal skulls onto some of their fenceposts in hopes of warding off the witches. As for the Skinwalker Ranch property, which borders the Ute Reservation, allegedly no Ute will dare set foot on it.

But why the curse on the Utes? The Utes' history with the Navajo is a complicated one. Initially, the Utes and Navajos would occasionally align to defeat common enemies. That all changed when the Utes themselves began to subjugate the Navajos and sell them on the slave markets in New Mexico prior to the Civil War. During the Civil War, some of the Utes aligned themselves with Kit Carson in his military campaign against the Navajo. Ever since then, the Navajo have despised the Ute, which led to the Ute belief that the Navajos cursed them with a plague of skinwalkers. Specifically, the Utes seem to believe in one head skinwalker that lives in a spot not far from the ranch called Dark Canyon. Supposedly in Dark Canyon can be found ancient petroglyphs depicting said skinwalker. However, all academic requests to see the petroglyphs have been denied by the tribal government who fear the skinwalker to this day. However, all that said, the counter argument is that even the Navajo wouldn't trust skinwalkers or make any type of deal with them to begin with.

UTE TRIBE POSSIBLY IN COLORADO OR UTAH.

In compiling this book, I had hoped to perhaps unearth some bonafide Wild West era Skinwalker Ranch stories. Unfortunately, I wasn't able to do so myself. However, researchers Gary and Wendy Swanson have made it a mission of theirs in recent years to collect skinwalker lore from the region. Their book, *Skinwalker: Guardian of the Last Portal*, tells of some of the earlier encounters on Skinwalker Ranch back when it was owned by the Myers. A witness, 84 years old at the time of the book's publication in 2020, wrote to the Swansons to tell them how he and his cousin would sneak onto Old Man Meyers' ranch to camp. They managed to sneak past Meyers' watchful eye by taking a little raft up the river to camp within a canyon. While there, they observed a glowing ball of light float through the air, which was very similar to sightings had by the Shermans years later.

THE MASONIC CONNECTION?

In addition to Native American lore, the Skinwalker Ranch is also tied to Masonic mysticism in a very unexpected way. Though the Masons were mostly associated with well-to-do Anglo men back in the 19th Century, there were also African American chapters. At Fort Duchesne near the Ute reservation were a group of Masonic Buffalo soldiers as it turns out. It's possible that this Masonic Chapter carved a Masonic symbol along Skinwalker Ridge. It was carved in a precarious place, as though the carver would have to be hung upside down to do so as it's several feet below the top of the ridge. Why they carved it there is a mystery, but to this day, the Utes recall the Masonic rites practiced by the Buffalo Soldiers. They should since many modern Ute homes are built over the graveyard of the Buffalo Soldiers of Fort Duchesne and are said to be haunted. Also worth mentioning is a water filled ravine called Bottle Hollow (because the soldiers used to toss their bottle caps into it). The ravine was filled with water in 1970 and is haunted by a spectral water serpent that is said to have killed several people. Bottle Hollow runs right along the Skinwalker Ranch, and considering the ranch has UFO and werewolf sightings, why not a water monster as well?

While this in of itself wasn't terribly interesting, it did lead to the boys asking their elders about the ranch. Reportedly, some of the scuttlebutt was that the "ranchers used to say that werewolves lived up [on the ridge]!"[84] One of the boys' fathers also

---

[84] Swanson, *Skinwalker: Guardian of the Last Portal*, p.79.

recalled seeing the glowing orbs back in his day when he would hunt deer in the area. Furthermore, he said that the orbs would scare off the cattle. The 84-year-old man who wrote the Swansons also recalled "three different instances where cattle on three separate ranches had been found dead..."[85] The man went on to relate that there were no signs of what killed the cattle. It also wasn't limited to the Myers ranch and extended to two other ranches. "[I]t put fear into the ranchers, and it was what all the kids talked about over at the school, because it was really scary."[86] The animals had been gutted, which struck everyone as strange since a predator would have gone for the meaty parts of the cow, but not the inner organs. This was, of course, prior to the widespread cattle mutilations of the 1970s. Judging by the 84-year-old witness saying that they were in school at the time, the story likely took place in the 1940s. "I remember my own father and his brother, my uncle, talking about it because my uncle also lost one cow. My uncle said the cow's tail was gone as well as her ears, and something or someone had also cut off her eyelids!"[87]

The man said that after the mutilation incidents he quit camping at the Myers Place. He also heard reports of one of the Myers ranch hands shooting at some type of strange creature to no avail. Apparently, some of these deaths were blamed on the Navajo. The witness wrote, "...the rancher's

---

[85] Ibid.
[86] Ibid.
[87] Ibid.

association was going out in different posses after what they called the 'Skinwalker witches.' They were suddenly convinced that the Navajo tribe south of us had created this witch to run the whites and Utes out of the area."[88]

Of course, we have to entertain the notion that the teller of this tale may have read about the notorious Skinwalker Ranch and decided to make up a story about it. While technically that is a possibility, it still wouldn't surprise me at all to find out that it was true. If anything bothers me personally about the Skinwalker Ranch's credibility, it's that strangely enough, so far no one seems to have found any record from the Myers themselves alleging paranormal activity on their ranch.[89]

In fact, in a memoir, Edith Myers described the ranch as "paradise" and lived alone there for several years after the death of her husband, Kenneth. This seems odd since the Sherman family who owned the ranch were terrified to be there one at a time. Why was this? Were the Myers under some form of spiritual protection not afforded the Shermans years later? Did the Myers perhaps have supernatural incidents and encounters and simply chose not to talk about them? Or, for the most far out theory, and also my favorite, were the Myers in some way in on and

---

[88] Ibid, p.80.

[89] Remember, the account just given purports to tell of the Myers shooting at Skinwalkers, but it did not come from the Myers themselves, so it should still be taken with a grain of salt.

complacent with the secret of what would one day be known as Skinwalker Ranch?

If the accounts of the Shermans as published in the breakthrough book, 2005's *Hunt for the Skinwalker*, are true, then the latter theory just might be right. According to the Shermans, when they acquired the ranch, they took note of the many double locks and heavy-duty latches on all the ranch doors and windows, as though the Myers had been fearful of something outside. In *Hunt for the Skinwalker*, Colm A. Kelleher and George Knapp wrote:

> When the [Shermans] first entered the small ranch house that was to be their home, they felt a chill. Every door had several large, heavy-duty dead bolts on both the inside and outside. All of the windows were bolted, and at each end of the farmhouse, large metal chains attached to huge steel rings were embedded securely into the wall. The previous owners had apparently chained very large guard dogs on both ends of the house. And they had barred the windows and put dead bolts on both sides of each door.[90]

Furthermore, there was a strange clause in the real estate contract that stated that the former owners were to be notified of any digging on the property. This brings to mind fears of disturbing Native American burial grounds. Gwen Sherman

---

[90] Kelleher and Knapp, *Hunt for the Skinwalker*, pp.10-11.

told Ryan Skinner, author of *Digging Into Skinwalker Ranch,* the following as well,

> When Garth Myers the executor of the estate of Ken and Edith Myers sold us the Ranch, he never mentioned anything to us about what was going on there. All he did was instruct us not to dig with a backhoe or move the big rock by the middle Homestead that appeared to have rolled off the hill.[91]

So what are we to make of the werewolves that skulk across the ground while UFOs streak through the skies of Skinwalker Ranch? Although these ties between Native American curses and aliens from other worlds may seem to be strange bedfellows, one shouldn't forget that nearly all Native Americans have legends of "other worlds." However, in their context, other worlds typically meant portals into alternate dimensions and parallel realities.

In fact, the Shermans occasionally employed a Native American ranch hand who had these beliefs. This man wrote to the Swansons to tell that according to what he knew from his own experience and others in the area that the ranch served as a gateway to a parallel dimension. According to the man, the previous owners, presumably the Myers, knew where these dividers between worlds were and carefully built their

---

[91] Skinner, *Digging Into Skinwalker Ranch*, p.39.

fences along them so that no one passed into them accidentally. The man wrote that,

> ...[the ranch] was rumored to be haunted by evil spirits from the dark world that existed alongside ours. Everyone said that this area where the ranch was located was along an "invisible, thin wall." Which, if one were not careful, they could easily bump into it and fall through the wall into another world! Everyone that I ever spoke with about that wall had the same fear of that other parallel world.[92]

The ranch hand said that he knew an elder tribesman who claimed that if a person were to stand by that "invisible wall" that everything would appear to be of a normal landscape until after a person walked through it. The man then went on to claim that voices could be heard coming from the portal, begging for help, a common skinwalker tactic.

And strange though it may seem, even the floating balls of light tie into skinwalker lore. In Native American belief systems and Spanish New Mexico folklore both, witches were said to either ride fireballs or turn into fireballs to travel through the air. New Mexico is rife with folktales and allegedly true sightings alike of glowing orbs of light purported to be witches. This, too, applies to the skinwalker in some instances, which is said to be

---

[92] Swanson, *The Last Skinwalker: The Avenging Witch Of The Navajo Nation*, p.59.

able to turn into an orb of light and fly in some traditions.

So, even though there is that small tie between Southwest witchcraft and lights in the sky, the question still lingers, what is Skinwalker Ranch? Is it simply land cursed by Navajo skinwalkers, or is it perhaps the gateway to another dimension? Forteans for years have spoken of such places, or realms perhaps we should call them. Some call this hidden realm Magonia, others Etheria, but whatever you call it, it seems to lead to an unseen dimension inhabited by monsters and other strange beings. In the words of Jacques Vallée, the Skinwalker Ranch does indeed appear to be a "passport to Magonia".

Sources:

Kelleher, Colm A. and George Knapp. *Hunt for the Skinwalker.* Pocket Books, 2005.

Skinner, Ryan and Cheryl Lynn Carter. *Digging Into Skinwalker Ranch.* Skinner Enterprises LLC, 2021.

Swanson, Gary and Wendy. *The Last Skinwalker: The Avenging Witch Of The Navajo Nation.* By the authors, 2018.

------------------------------------- *Skinwalker: Guardian of the Last Portal.* By the authors, 2020.

AFTERWORD

Most of you know me from the *Cowboys & Saurians* series, of which this book is technically a part, devoted to remnant dinosaurs and monstrous creatures sighted during North America's Pioneer Period. Most of you also probably knew that this day would come, that being the day that I finally ran out of dinosaurs and started scraping the bottom of the barrel for anything I could find to milk another book out of the series. Well, you're wrong. I'm not out of dinosaurs, not by a long shot. I just decided to let them take a break for a while to focus on something a little different in the form of these creatures of the night. (The dinosaurs will return soon enough in a volume devoted to saurian sightings in the Outback of Australia.)

And, actually, I'm not done with the creatures of the night either. As I was compiling this volume, like the gelatinous red monster of 1957's *The Blob*, this tome kept growing and growing until it was well over 500 pages with no end in sight. As I discovered the great range of stories devoted to each the vampires, the werewolves, and the mummies, I decided that each could carry their own volume respectively.

For a while, I even considered just launching a new series and doing that alone. However, I really liked the idea of a book that had all three—vampires, mummies and werewolves—plus a few other spooks like the Banshee of the Badlands, Spring Heeled Jack, and others. So, I decided to have my cake and eat it too. This book would serve as the fifth volume in the *Cowboys & Saurians* series after all while also launching its own series, which will be branded as *Cowboys & Monsters*.

The best is yet to come, so stay tuned for more vampires, mummies, and werewolves of the Wild West!

ACKNOWLEDGMENTS

A big thank you to my author pals David Weatherly, who helped me find some extra werewolf stories, and Donna Blake Birchell, who scanned this book's first draft to remind me of anything I might've missed—mainly the mummy of Elmer McCurdy. As always, at least half of these books' success in luring you in, dear reader, is talented cover artist Jolyon Yates, who always knocks them out of the park!

INDEX

ABOUT THE AUTHOR

John LeMay was born and raised in Roswell, NM, the "UFO Capital of the World." He is the author of over 35 books on film and western history such as *Kong Unmade: The Lost Films of Skull Island*, *Tall Tales and Half Truths of Billy the Kid*, and *Roswell USA: Towns That Celebrate UFOs, Lake Monsters, Bigfoot and Other Weirdness*. He is also the editor/publisher of *The Lost Films Fanzine* and has written for magazines such as *True West*, *Cinema Retro*, and *Mad Scientist* to name only a few. He is a Past President of the Board of Directors for the Historical Society for Southeast New Mexico and the host of the web series *Roswell's Hidden History*.

THE BICEP BOOKS CATALOGUE

The following titles are available for purchase on Amazon.com, and are available to bookstores at a wholesale discount via Ingram Content Group (ISBNs of available editions listed for this purpose)

THE BIG BOOK OF JAPANESE GIANT MONSTER MOVIES SERIES

The third edition of the book that started it all! Reviews over 100 tokusatsu films between 1954 and 1988. All the Godzilla, Gamera, and Daimajin movies made during the Showa era are covered plus lesser known fare like *Invisible Man vs. The Human Fly* (1957) and *Conflagration* (1975). Softcover (380 pp/5.83" X 8.27") Suggested Retail: $19.99 SBN:978-1-7341546-4-1

This third edition reviews over 75 tokusatsu films between 1989 and 2019. All the Godzilla, Gamera, and Ultraman movies made during the Heisei era are covered plus independent films like *Reigo, King of the Sea Monsters* (2005), *Demcking, the Sea Monster* (2009) and *Attack of the Giant Teacher* (2019)! Softcover (260 pp/5.83" X 8.27") Suggested Retail: $19.99 ISBN: 978-1- 7347816-4-9

This second edition of the Rondo Award nominated book covers un-produced scripts like *Bride of Godzilla* (1955), partially shot movies like *Giant Horde Beast Nezura* (1963), and banned films like *Prophecies of Nostradamus* (1974), plus hundreds of other lost productions. Softcover/Hard-cover (470pp. /7" X 10") Suggested Retail: $24.99 (sc)/$39.95(hc)ISBN: 978-1-73 41546-0-3 (hc)

This sequel to *The Lost Films* covers the non-giant monster unmade movie scripts from Japan such as *Frankenstein vs. the Human Vapor* (1963), *After Japan Sinks* (1974-76), plus lost movies like *Fearful Attack of the Flying Saucers* (1956) and *Venus Flytrap* (1968). Hardcover (200 pp/5.83" X 8.27")/Softcover (216 pp/ 5.5" X 8.5") Suggested Retail: $9.99 (sc)/$24.99(hc) ISBN:978-1-7341546 -3-4 (hc)

This companion book to *The Lost Films* charts the development of all the prominent Japanese monster movies including discarded screenplays, story ideas, and deleted scenes. Also includes bios for writers like Shinichi Sekizawa, Niisan Takahashi and many others. Comprehensive script listing and appendices as well. Hardcover/Softcover (370 pp./ 6"X9") Suggested Retail: $16.95(sc)/$34.99(hc)ISBN: 978-1-7341546-5-8 (hc)

Examines the differences between the U.S. and Japanese versions of over 50 different tokusatsu films like *Gojira* (1954)/*Godzilla, King of the Monsters!* (1956), *Gamera* (1965)/ *Gammera, the Invincible* (1966), *Submersion of Japan* (1973)/*Tidal Wave* (1975), and many, many more! Softcover (540 pp./ 6"X9") Suggested Retail: $22.99 ISBN: 978-1-953221-77 -3

Examines the differences between the European and Japanese versions of tokusatsu films including the infamous "Cozzilla" colorized version of *Godzilla*, from 1977, plus rarities like *Terremoto 10 Grado*, the Italian cut of *Legend of Dinosaurs*. The book also examines the condensed Champion Matsuri edits of Toho's effects films. Softcover (372 pp./ 6"X9") Suggested Retail: $19.99 ISBN: 978-1- 953221-77-3

Throughout the 1960s and 1970s the Italian film industry cranked out over 600 "Spaghetti Westerns" and for every *Fistful of Dollars* were a dozen pale imitations, some of them hilarious. Many of these lesser known Spaghettis are available in bargain bin DVD packs and stream for free online. If ever you've wondered which are worth your time and which aren't, this is the book for you. Softcover (160pp./5.06" X 7.8") Suggested Retail: $9.99

THE BICEP BOOKS CATALOGUE

CLASSIC MONSTERS SERIES

Kong Unmade explores unproduced scripts like *King Kong vs. Frankenstein* (1958), unfinished films like *The Lost Island* (1934), and lost movies like *King Kong Appears in Edo* (1938). As a bonus, all the Kong rip-offs like *Konga* (1961) and *Queen Kong* (1976) are reviewed. Hardcover (350 pp/5.83" X 8.27")/Softcover (376 pp/ 5.5" X 8.5") Suggested Retail: $24.99 (hc)/$19.99(sc) ISBN: 978-1-7341546-2-7(hc)

Jaws Unmade explores unproduced scripts like *Jaws 3, People 0* (1979), abandoned ideas like a Quint prequel, and even aborted sequels to Jaws inspired movies like *Orca Part II*. As a bonus, all the Jaws rip-offs like *Grizzly* (1976) and *Tentacles* (1977) are reviewed. Hardcover (316 pp/5.83" X 8.27")/Softcover (340 pp/5.5" X 8.5") Suggested Retail: $29.99 (hc)/$17.95(sc) ISBN: 978-1-7344730-1-8

Classic Monsters Unmade covers lost and unmade films starring Dracula, Frankenstein, the Mummy and more monsters. Reviews unmade scripts like *The Return of Frankenstein* (1934) and *Wolf Man vs. Dracula* (1944). It also examines lost films of the silent era such as *The Werewolf* (1913) and *Drakula's Death* (1923). Softcover/Hardcover(428pp/5.83"X8.27") Suggested Retail: $22.99(sc)/$27.99(hc)ISBN:978-1-953221-85-8(hc)

Volume 2 explores the Hammer era and beyond, from unmade versions of *Brides of Dracula* (called *Disciple of Dracula*) to remakes of *Creature from the Black Lagoon*. Completely unmade films like *Kali: Devil Bride of Dracula* (1975) and *Godzilla vs. Frankenstein* (1964) are covered along with lost completed films like *Batman Fights Dracula* (1967) and *Black the Ripper* (1974). Coming Fall 2021.

NOSTALGIA

Written in the same spirit as *The Big Book of Japanese Giant Monster Movies*, this tome reviews all the classic Universal and Hammer horrors like Dracula, Frankenstein, the Gillman and the rest along with obscure flicks like *The New Invisible Man* (1958), *Billy the Kid versus Dracula* (1966), *Blackenstein* (1973) and *Legend of the Werewolf* (1974). Softcover (394 pp/5.5" X 8.5") Suggested Retail: $17.95

Written at an intermediate reading level for the kid in all of us, these picture books will take you back to your youth. In the spirit of the old Ian Thorne books are covered *Nabonga* (1944), *White Pongo* (1945) and more! Hardcover/Softcover (44 pp/7.5" X 9.25") Suggested Retail: $17.95(hc)/$9.99(sc) ISBN: 978-1-7341546-9-6 (hc) 978-1-7344730-5-6 (sc)

Written at an intermediate reading level for the kid in all of us, these picture books will take you back to your youth. In the spirit of the old Ian Thorne books are covered *The Lost World* (1925), *Land That Time Forgot* (1975) and more! Hardcover/Softcover (44 pp/7.5" X 9.25") Retail: $17.95 (hc)/$9.99(sc) ISBN: 978-1-7344730-6-3 (hc) 978-1-7344730-7-0 (sc)

Written at an intermediate reading level for the kid in all of us, these picture books will take you back to your youth. In the spirit of the old Ian Thorne books covered *Them!* (1954), *Empire of the Ants* (1977) and more! Hardcover/Softcover (44 pp/7.5" X 9.25") Suggested Retail: $17.95(hc)/$9.99(sc) ISBN: 978-1-7347816-3-2 (hc) 978-1-7347816-2-5 (sc)

THE BICEP BOOKS CATALOGUE

CRYPTOZOOLOGY/COWBOYS & SAURIANS

Cowboys & Saurians: Prehistoric Beasts as Seen by the Pioneers explores dinosaur sightings from the pioneer period via real newspaper reports from the time. Well-known cases like the Tombstone Thunderbird are covered along with more obscure cases like the Crosswicks Monster and more. Softcover (357 pp/5.06" X 7.8"] Suggested Retail: $19.95 ISBN: 978-1-7341546-1-0

Cowboys & Saurians: Ice Age zeroes in on snowbound saurians like the Ceratosaurus of the Arctic Circle and a Tyrannosaurus of the Tundra, as well as sightings of Ice Age megafauna like mammoths, glyptodonts, Sarkastodons and Saber-toothed tigers. Tales of a land that time forgot in the Arctic are also covered. Softcover (264 pp/5.06" X 7.8") Suggested Retail: $14.99 ISBN: 978-1-7341546-7-2

Southerners & Saurians takes the series formula of exploring newspaper accounts of monsters in the pioneer period with an eye to the Old South. In addition to dinosaurs are covered Lizardmen, Frogmen, giant leeches and mosquitoes, and the Dingocroc, which might be an alien rather than a prehistoric survivor. Softcover (202 pp/5.06" X 7.8"] Suggested Retail: $13.99 ISBN: 978-1-7344730-4-9

Cowboys & Saurians South of the Border explores the saurians of Central and South America, like the Patagonian Plesiosaurus that was really an Iemisch, plus tales of the Neo-Mylodon, a menacing monster from underground called the Minhocao, Glyptodonts, and even Bolivia's three-headed dinosaur! Softcover (412 pp/ 5.06"X7.8") Suggested Retail: $17.95 ISBN: 978-1-953221-73-5

UFOLOGY/THE REAL COWBOYS & ALIENS IN CONJUNCTION WITH ROSWELL BOOKS

The Real Cowboys and Aliens: Early American UFOs explores UFO sightings in the USA between the years 1800-1864. Stories of encounters sometimes involved famous figures in U.S. history such as Lewis and Clark, and Thomas Jefferson.Hardcover (242pp/6" X 9") Softcover (262 pp/5.06" X 7.8") Suggested Retail: $24.99 (hc)/$15.95\(sc) ISBN: 978-1-7341546-8-9\(hc)/978-1-7344 730-8-7(sc)

The second entry in the series, *Old West UFOs*, covers reports spanning the years 1865-1895. Includes tales of Men in Black, Reptilians, Spring-Heeled Jack, Sasquatch from space, and other alien beings, in addition to the UFOs and airships. Hardcover (276 pp/6" X 9") Softcover (308 pp/5.06" X 7.8") Suggested Retail: $29.95 (hc)/$17.95(sc) ISBN: 978-1-7344730-0-1 (hc)/ 978-1-73447 30-2-5 (sc)

The third entry in the series, *The Coming of the Airships*, encompasses a short time frame with an incredibly high concentration of airship sightings between 1896-1899. The famous Aurora, Texas, UFO crash of 1897 is covered in depth along with many others. Hardcover (196 pp/6" X 9") Softcover (222 pp/5.06" X 7.8") Suggested Retail: $24.99 (hc)/$15.95(sc) ISBN: 978-1-7347816 -1-8 (hc)/978-1-7347816-0-1(sc)

Early 20th Century UFOs kicks off a new series that investigates UFO sightings of the early 1900s. Includes tales of UFOs sighted over the *Titanic* as it sank, Nikola Tesla receiving messages from the stars, an alien being found encased in ice, and a possible virus from outer space!Hardcover (196 pp/6" X 9") Softcover (222 pp/5.06" X 7.8") Suggested Retail: $27.99 (hc)/$16.95(sc) ISBN: 978-1-7347816-1-8 (hc)/978-1-73478 16-0-1(sc)

LOST FILMS FANZINE BACK ISSUES

THE LOST FILMS FANZINE VOL.1

ISSUE #1 SPRING 2020 The lost Italian cut of *Legend of Dinosaurs and Monster Birds* called *Terremoto 10 Grado*, plus *Bride of Dr. Phibes* script, *Good Luck! Godzilla*, the King Kong remake that became a car comm ercial, Bollywood's lost *Jaws* rip-off, Top Ten Best Fan Made Godzilla trailers plus an interview with Scott David Lister. 60 pages. Three variant covers/editions (premium color/basic color/b&w)

ISSUE #2 SUMMER 2020 How 1935's *The Capture of Tarzan* became 1936's *Tarzan Escapes*, the Orca sequels that weren't, Baragon in Bollywood's *One Million B.C.*, unmade *Kolchak: The Night Stalker* movies, *The Norliss Tapes*, *Superman V: The New Movie*, why there were no *Curse of the Pink Panther* sequels, *Moonlight Mask: The Movie*. 64 pages. Two covers/editions (basic color/b&w)

ISSUE #3 FALL 2020 Blob sequels both forgotten and unproduced, *Horror of Dracula* uncut, *Frankenstein Meets the Wolfman* and talks, myths of the lost *King Kong* Spider-Pit sequence debunked, the *Carnosaur* novel vs. the movies, *Terror in the Streets* 50th anniversary, *Bride of Godzilla* 55th Unniversary, Lee Powers sketchbook. 100 pages. Two covers/editions (basic color/b&w)

ISSUE #4 WINTER 2020/21 *Diamonds Are Forever*'s first draft with Goldfinger, *Disciple of Dracula* into *Brides of Dracula*, *War of the Worlds* That Weren't Part II, *Day the Earth Stood Still II* by Ray Bradbury, *Deathwish 6*, *Atomic War Bride*, *What Am I Doing in the Middle of a Revolution?*, *Spring Dream in the Old Capital* and more. 70 pages. Two covers/editions (basic color/b&w)

THE LOST FILMS FANZINE VOL.2

ISSUE #5 SPRING 2021 The lost films and projects of ape suit performer Charles Gemora, plus *Superman Reborn*, *Teenage Mutant Ninja Turtles IV: The Next Mutation*, *Mikado Zombie*, NBC's *Big Stuffed Dog*, King Ghidorah flies solo, *Grizzly II* reviewed, and War of the Worlds That Weren't concludes with a musical. Plus Blu-Ray reviews, news, and letters. 66 pages. Two covers/editions (basic color/ b&w)

ISSUE #6 SUMMER 2021 Peter Sellers *Romance of the Pink Panther*, Akira Kurosawa's *Song of the Horse*, *Kali - Devil Bride of Dracula*, Jack Black as Green Lantern, *Ladybug, Ladybug, The Lost Atlantis*, Japan's lost superhero Hiyo Man, and *Lord of Light*, the CIA's covert movie that inspired 2012's *Argo*. Plus news, Blu-Ray reviews, and letters. 72 pages. Two covers/editions (basic color/b&w)

ISSUE #7 FALL 2021 *Hiero's Journey*, Don Bragg in *Tarzan and the Jewels of Opar*, DC's *Lobo* movie, Lee Powers Scrapbook returns, Blake Matthews uncovers *The Big Boss Part II* (1976), Matthew B. Lamont searches for lost Three Stooges, and an ape called Kong in 1927's *Isle of Sunken Gold*. Plus news, and letters. 72 pages. Two covers/editions (basic color /b&w)

ISSUE #8 WINTER 2021/22 The connection between Steve Reeves' unmade third Hercules movie and *Goliath and the Dragon*, *The Iron Man* starring Tom Cruise, Phil Yordan's *King Kong* remake, *The Unearthly Stranger*, Saturday Supercade forgotten cartoon, the 45th anniversary of Luigi Cozzi's "Cozzilla" and *Day the Earth Froze*. Plus news and letters. 72 pages. Two covers/editions (basic color /b&w)

MOVIE MILESTONES BACK ISSUES

MOVIE MILESTONES VOL. 1   VOL. 2

ISSUE #1 AUGUST 2020 Debut issue celebrating 80 years of *One Million B.C.* (1940), and an early 55th Anniversary for *One Million Years B.C.* (1966). Abandoned ideas, casting changes, and deleted scenes are covered, plus, a mini-B.C. stock-footage filmography and much more! 54 pages. Three collectible covers/editions (premium color/basic color/b&w)

ISSUE #2 OCTOBER 2020 Celebrates the joint 50th Anniversaries of *When Dinosaurs Ruled the Earth* (1970) and *Creatures the World Forgot* (1971). Also includes looks at *Prehistoric Women* (1967), *When Women Had Tails* (1970), and *Caveman* (1981), plus unmade films like *When the World Cracked Open*. 72 pages. Three collectible covers/editions (premium color/basic color/b&w)

ISSUE #3 WINTER 2021 Japanese 'Panic Movies' like *The Last War* (1961), *Submersion of Japan* (1973), and *Bullet Train* (1975) are covered on celebrated author Sakyo Komatsu's 90th birthday. The famous banned Toho film *Prophecies of Nostradamus* (1974) are also covered. 124 pages. Three collectible covers/editions (premium color/ basic color/ b&w)

ISSUE #4 SPRING 2021 This issue celebrates the joint 60th Anniversaries of *Gorgo*, *Reptilicus* and *Konga* examining unmade sequels like *Reptilicus 2*, and other related lost projects like *Kuru Island* and *The Volcano Monsters*. Also explores the Gorgo, Konga and Reptilicus comic books from Charlton. 72 pages. Three collectible covers/editions (premium color/basic color/b&w)

MOVIE MILESTONES VOL. 2   VOL. 3 COMING SOON

ISSUE #5 SUMMER 2021 *Godzilla vs. the Sea Monster* gets the spotlight, with an emphasis on its original version *King Kong vs. Ebirah*, plus information on *The King Kong Show* which inspired it, and Jun Fukuda's tangentially related spy series *100 Shot/100 Killed*. 72 pages. Three collectible covers/editions (premium color /basic color/b&w)

ISSUE #6 FALL 2021 Monster Westerns of the 1950s and 1960s are spotlighted in the form of *Teenage Monster*, *The Curse of the Undead*, *Billy the Kid Versus Dracula*, *Jesse James Meets Frankenstein's Daughter*, and Bela Lugosi's unmade *The Ghoul Goes West*. 50 pages. Special Black and White exclusive!

ISSUE #7 WINTER 2022 This issue is all about Amicus's Edgar Rice Burroughs trilogy including *Land That Time Forgot*, *At the Earth's Core*, *People That Time Forgot* plus unmade sequels like *Out of Time's Abyss* or *Doug McClure as John Carter of Mars*. All this plus *Warlords of Atlantis* and *Arabian Adventure*! 100 pages. Three collectible covers/editions (premium color /basic color/b&w)

ISSUE #8 SPRING 2022 *Godzilla vs. Gigan* turns 50 and this issue is here to celebrate with its many unmade versions, like *Godzilla vs. the Space Monsters* and *Return of King Ghidorah*, plus *The Mysterians* 65th anniversary and *Daigoro vs. Goliath's* 50th.

Printed in Great Britain
by Amazon